D0535277

*Leadership
by
Design*

Leadership
by
Design

Strengthening Integrity
in Higher Education

E. Grady Bogue

NATIONAL UNIVERSITY
LIBRARY   SAN DIEGO

Jossey-Bass Publishers • San Francisco

Copyright © 1994 by Jossey-Bass Inc., Publishers, 350 Sansome Street, San Francisco, California 94104. Copyright under International, Pan American, and Universal Copyright Conventions. All rights reserved. No part of this book may be reproduced in any form—except for brief quotation (not to exceed 1,000 words) in a review or professional work—without permission in writing from Jossey-Bass Inc., Publishers, 350 Sansome Street, San Francisco, California 94104.

Substantial discounts on bulk quantities of Jossey-Bass books are available to corporations, professional associations, and other organizations. For details and discount information, contact the special sales department at Jossey-Bass Inc., Publishers. (415) 433-1740; Fax (415) 433-0499.

For international orders, please contact your local Paramount Publishing International office.

Manufactured in the United States of America. Nearly all Jossey-Bass books and jackets are printed on recycled paper that contains at least 50 percent recycled waste, including 10 percent postconsumer waste. Many of our materials are also printed with vegetable-based inks; during the printing process these inks emit fewer volatile organic compounds (VOCs) than petroleum-based inks. VOCs contribute to the formation of smog.

Library of Congress Cataloging-in-Publication Data

Bogue, E. Grady (Ernest Grady), date.
    Leadership by design : strengthening integrity in higher education / E. Grady Bogue — 1st ed.
        p.   cm.—(The Jossey-Bass higher and adult education series)
    Includes bibliographical references (p.   ) and index.
    ISBN 0-7879-0034-6
    1. College administrators—United States.   2. Leadership—United States.   I. Title.   II. Series.
LB2341.B554   1994
378.1′07—dc20   94-22145
                                                                              CIP

FIRST EDITION
HB Printing   10 9 8 7 6 5 4 3 2 1   *Code 94115*

The Jossey-Bass
Higher and Adult Education Series

Contents

Contents

Preface

As evidenced in literary works from Plato's *Republic* and Machiavelli's *The Prince* to Burns's *Leadership* and Gardner's *On Leadership*, probably no aspect of human behavior has been subjected to such intensive empirical and philosophical inquiry as has the aspect of leadership. There is an informing general literature and a helpful one on leadership in collegiate settings. Among the volumes devoted to this topic in colleges and universities are Donald Walker's *The Effective Administrator* (1979) and Robert Birnbaum's *How Academic Leadership Works* (1992). This literature embraces a range of themes, from ethics to effectiveness, from culture to charisma.

And who would discount the abundant literature in which themes and ideas complement, and often anticipate, the power of ideas found in professional works? From the pages of biography and history, poetry and plays, essays and personal letters, flow lessons both instructive and inspiring to those with leadership responsibilities.

Nevertheless, some collegiate leaders disdain the need to know anything about the definition of their role, the exercise of authority, the anatomy of decision, the sources of motivation, and the forms of organization. An absence of curiosity about how we can utilize ideas and research for the improvement of leadership performance must be counted a disappointing posture for those holding climates of learning in trust.

A few collegiate leaders would appear to suffer not only from a poverty of ideas but from a poverty of ideals as well. That something is missing not only in the minds but in the hearts of some contemporary collegiate leaders is immediately apparent to anyone who reads the *Chronicle of Higher Education* with any regularity. Here we can read of the most surprising, disappointing, and occasionally bizarre leadership behaviors—of chairs, deans, vice presidents, and presidents placing their clients and colleagues, their organizations and institutions, in harm's way. It is almost impossible to read a single week of the *Chronicle* without finding a record of college leaders betraying personal, professional, and public trust. Moreover, stories of scandal and betrayal in collegiate settings are not restricted to professional publications. We are as likely to find them in the *New York Times*, the *Wall Street Journal*, or one of the weekly news magazines.

The Purpose of the Book

Of course, no one will argue, nor do I imply, that these departures from standards of nobility and integrity constitute the *dominant* reality, which is the goodness that is exhibited every day in every college and university in the United States. What might be argued and what I suggest as a major thesis of this book, however, is that even one collegiate leader who abandons the call of honor, whose conscience betrays his or her competence, is one too many, and that every departure damages the entire enterprise. A dimension of my thesis is therefore that the principal challenge to leadership effectiveness in colleges and universities is more than a challenge of intellect—to acquire and use good ideas. It is a challenge of character—to learn and apply constructive ideals.

We might initially be drawn to a vision of colleges and universities as places of nobility and rationality, which they certainly should be. Such a limited perspective, however, is bland and fails to present the complexity and multiple realities of the collegiate enterprise. Colleges and universities are not structural, symbolic, and social configurations free from love and license, sacrifice and selfishness, passion and prejudice, morality and meanness.

In the September 25, 1991, issue of the *Chronicle of Higher Education*, there appeared a sad story of collegiate administration. Two Washington attorneys were interviewed about their experience with university administrators. One of the attorneys responded that "the word that comes to mind is 'pathetic'. . . . They're easily mau maued. They don't want trouble. Above all, they want to keep the university out of the papers, and they don't stand for anything" (Magner, 1991, p. A5). To be accused of having an empty mind and heart must be the ultimate insult for anyone who would claim to have leadership responsibility in our colleges and universities. I shared this article with my students at the University of Tennessee and advised that if anyone, especially an attorney, ever remarked that one of them did not stand for anything, I would try to have his or her degree recalled.

What should leaders stand for? What are the ideals that both research and reflection tell us are more likely to yield constructive and effective leadership behavior? And what are the ideals that will enable us to design environments in which our colleagues and our colleges reach the far edge of their promise, that will enable us to nurture the potential of our students and our other clients? The titles of the reflective chapters in this book telegraph my response to these questions: "The Call of Honor," "The Dignity Test," "The Habit of Curiosity," "The Case for Candor," "The Touch of Compassion," "The Question of Courage," "The Expectation of Excellence," and "The Servant Exemplar."

Each chapter centers on a design ideal. Here, then, is another element of my thesis in this book: leaders are designers. With our theories, we can imprison and defeat, or we can free and elevate the human mind and spirit. These ideals do not require collegiate leaders to forsake the beautiful edges of their personality, the elements of touch and style that make them memorable and effective. They do not require a foolish and Pollyanna belief that does not take into account the presence of both nobility and meanness even in the collegiate domain. Nor do they require a slavish consistency that ignores the power of surprise and the salutary power of guerrilla goodness—the use of unorthodox tactics in the service of worthy goals—in combating violations of and challenges to a leader's trust and compassion.

Leaders have a special freedom and responsibility as designers, because their design is never really finished. Equity, diversity, and freedom—all worthy design ideals—must be balanced with justice, community, and responsibility. It is in the practice of leadership that our design ideals become manifest. To paraphrase a passage from Sophocles' *Antigone,* we will not know the heart of the leader until he or she is placed in a position of power. This volume is thus not about abstract design ideals but about their application in the practice and tactics of leadership.

The February 1994 issue of *Smithsonian* carries a cover picture of one of Frank Lloyd Wright's more famous home designs, Fallingwater. A picture accompanying the inside story shows Wright talking to some workers erecting scaffolding and pouring concrete on one of his projects. Designs have no elegance or power unless they work in practice. Leader values are not manifest in paper-and-pencil responses to value inventories but in how we live our lives. What is true in other art forms is also true of leadership.

Therefore, a third element of my thesis is that effective leadership is a conceptual, moral, and performing art form—one in which ideas and ideals are tested, integrated, and utilized in the act, the performance. An art form is not perfected in the passive mode, without the benefit of practice that leads to refinement of the performing skill. When technique is submerged and unconscious, when ideas are summoned to the fore almost without thought, when the discipline of previous practice produces without delay the appropriate response, when theory and fact are not burdens on the memory but constitute the instruments of our imagination and initiative, then we stand on the threshold of leadership art. It is in the application and practice of any art form that we create the "flow" of the art.

In these essays, I have tried to link the conceptual and the moral elements of leadership in a set of design ideals whose power and effectiveness can be demonstrated both philosophically and empirically to my satisfaction. Certainly, being an effective leader is more than being a good person. But from my philosophical perspective, one cannot be an effective leader without being a good person. The pervasive public cynicism that has arisen from the predictable and sour fruits of too many leaders who have abandoned their integrity is a testimony to this position.

Perfection is not what we seek or need in our leaders, collegiate, civic, or corporate. It is not what I seek to foster in this book. I want to assist leaders who have spiritual scars and calluses on their characters; these are the evidence that they have contended with moral issues of difficult demarcation, that they have weighed contending moral calls whose resolutions defy neat decision algorithms, that they have agonized over the guidance of their own conscience and the judgment of an opposing majority, that they have struggled to know what it means to answer the call of honor.

More than science and empirical theory are required of effective leadership in any organized enterprise, including university organizations. Effective leadership will be a construction of our values and ideals as well. Who will follow those who have no center of mind and heart? And to borrow a phrase from Joseph Conrad, who should follow those who have a "heart of darkness?" The most urgent business for the collegiate or any leader is the construction of a philosophy. An element of that philosophy will surely be that leadership is not necessarily something that others do for or to us, not something vested in a position; rather, it is what we accomplish together in shared ventures of purpose, persistence, and pleasure— a journey of shared ideals.

The Audience

Someone who suggests that there are already many good books on leadership (which apparently too many practicing collegiate leaders are ignoring) and who nevertheless writes another book to help treat this problem might justifiably be counted a candidate for therapeutic referral. Perhaps, however, the worth of these chapters may be established by their emphasis on the importance of leadership ideals.

In remarks before a variety of audiences and in my graduate classes, I have found that many individuals who hold the promise or reality of leadership responsibility—in our colleges and universities and in corporate and civic organizations—seem responsive to discussion concerning the ways in which our values construct our leadership realities. They are pleasantly surprised when public conversations move beyond objective theories, which undoubtedly have power to inform and improve our practice, to a consideration of how our ideas and our ideals interact to construct our theories in action.

The book is written for those academic administrators who try each day to answer the call of honor; I hope they will find it encouraging. It is written for those aspiring to collegiate leadership; I hope they will find it illuminating. It is intended for those who have been mentors for those now serving as collegiate leaders; I hope that they will find it affirming. It is written for those college leaders interested in enhancing their artistry and effectiveness; I hope they will find it stimulating. It is aimed at those who are developing and selecting our collegiate leaders; I hope they will remember to look for evidence of character and skill as well as academic pedigree. And it is written for leaders in corporate and civic sectors, who may find the stories of leading within the complex web of academic life of some value in exchanging a command-and-control design perspective for a servant and stewardship one. It is my hope that this book will enrich their understanding of both leadership and the beautiful and powerful instrument that is American higher education.

Acknowledgments

I would like to express appreciation to Gale Erlandson, editor of the Jossey-Bass Higher and Adult Education series, who encouraged me in this work and strengthened the manuscript with her deft editorial touch. Whatever imperfections and liabilities remain are my own. I thank Ann Richardson, editorial assistant at Jossey-Bass, for affirming and cheerful support throughout the preparation of the manuscript. I also thank Ms. Judy Barnes in the Department of Educational Leadership at the University of Tennessee for her care in reviewing and preparing the manuscript. For those friends who also reviewed this work—Susan Frost, John Prados, Carol Kasworm, and Wayne Andrews—I extend my heartfelt appreciation for their helpful contributions of candor and encouragement. Finally, I acknowledge the support of the University of Tennessee.

Dedication

I dedicate this work to two educators and collegiate leaders who
have been personal and professional friends, leadership mentors,
and scholarship partners in my life. They are servant exemplars,
who have effectively modeled the design ideals presented in this
book. To Dr. Robert L. Saunders and Dr. John K. Folger, leaders
who always answered the call of honor.

Knoxville, Tennessee   E. Grady Bogue
August 1994

The Author

E. Grady Bogue is a professor in the Department of Educational Leadership at the University of Tennessee and chancellor emeritus of Louisiana State University in Shreveport, where he served as chancellor for ten years. He received his B.S. degree (1957) in mathematics, his M.S. degree (1965) in education, and an Ed.D. degree in educational administration, all from Memphis State University. He served as interim chancellor of Louisiana State University and Agricultural and Mechanical College in 1989. From 1975 to 1980, he was associate director for the Tennessee Higher Education Commission. Between 1964 and 1974, he held three different administrative appointments at Memphis State, the last as assistant vice president for academic affairs. He was named a distinguished alumnus of Memphis State in 1986.

Bogue has written five books, and his articles have appeared in such journals as the *Harvard Business Review, Educational Record, Journal of Higher Education, Vital Speeches*, and *Phi Delta Kappan*. He has been a consultant on planning, evaluation, quality assurance, and leadership to colleges and universities, state-level higher education agencies, and corporations. He was an American Council on Education (ACE) fellow in academic administration in 1974–1975 and served as a visiting scholar with the Educational Testing Service in 1988–1989. During his ACE fellowship year and the following five years with the Tennessee Higher Education Commission, he was director of the Performance Funding Project, which developed and implemented one of the first state-level performance incentive policies in American higher education. He has been a visiting lecturer in China and is an adjunct member of the faculty at Northeast University in Shenyang, China.

*Leadership
by
Design*

1

The Call of Honor

There is a curious leadership context developing in higher education. On the one hand, we have more information available to guide collegiate leadership. As we saw in the Preface, an impressive array of volumes has appeared on this theme. In addition to these book-length treatments, several journals have recently featured full issues devoted to leadership topics. See, for example, the fall 1989 issue of the *NASPA Journal,* the winter 1991 issue of *National Forum,* and the fall 1992 issue of *Innovative Higher Education.* Two widely circulated monograph series also focus on these issues: *Making Sense of Administrative Leadership* in the 1989 *ASHE-ERIC Higher Education* reports and *Leaders on Leadership: The College Presidency,* a spring 1988 issue in the Jossey-Bass series New Directions for Higher Education. It can hardly be claimed, therefore, that there is a paucity of advice available to collegiate leaders.

On the other hand, the performance of some college leaders causes one to wonder whether this outpouring of information is doing any good. The college presidency would appear to be increasingly a place of difficult abode. In the 1991 annual report of the Commission on Colleges of the Southern Association of Colleges and Schools are sobering statistics on presidential turnover in southern institutions during the period 1986–1991 (Commission on Colleges, 1991). During this five-year period, the average turnover

1

rate approached 50 percent for the almost eight hundred colleges and universities composing the Commission on Colleges membership. My ten-and-a-half-year tenure as chancellor of Louisiana State University (LSU) in Shreveport appeared more satisfying as I noted that Louisiana had been a hazardous place for college presidents to live; the state had the highest turnover rate in the South at 56.7 percent. These regional statistics appear to be moderated by other reports indicating an average presidential tour of seven years, though the period of service is far shorter for presidents of state research universities. These statistics and others over the country reveal too many painful and premature exits.

Consider the conditions of presidential departure described in issues of the *Chronicle of Higher Education*. At Stanford University, President Donald Kennedy resigned following charges of mismanagement of federal research funds. At the University of Central Florida, according to the June 19, 1991, issue of the *Chronicle of Higher Education*, President Steven Altman's name was found on the client records of "massage" parlors in Orlando and apparently in several other cities around the country. Altman summarily resigned following the disclosure by Orlando newspapers. At Rockefeller University, President David Baltimore resigned over charges of falsified data in a research study. American University president Richard Berendzen pleaded guilty to the charge of making obscene phone calls from his office phone.

Whether many collegiate faculty and civic friends often read *GQ* magazine may be debated. I myself am not a regular reader; but in browsing through a bookstore in the summer of 1992, it was hard to ignore the story in the magazine entitled "Magna Cum Fraud." This was an account of Dr. James Holderman, former president of the University of South Carolina and former president emeritus (he was stripped of his emeritus title). Dr. Holderman was accused of using his office for personal gain and making sexual advances to male students working in his office (Cook, 1992). While Holderman's story had also appeared in several earlier issues of the *Chronicle of Higher Education*, the movement from professional to popular press could hardly be counted as good news for the image of higher education.

These and other tales of presidential misadventure certainly draw our attention to presidential performance, but they invite a deeper question as well. How did these collegiate leaders arrive at the presidential office? Was there a conceptual or ideological weakness that remained hidden to those making their appointment? Or did the challenges and pressures of the position create or expand character fissures in these leaders? The answer to these questions may evade precise answer but could involve both possibilities.

Let us also factor in the lively coverage associated with the departure financial arrangements for presidents who managed to exit of their own volition but who left behind them charges of lavish and inappropriate financial benefits associated with their departure. Following the furor associated with a departure package reputedly more than $3 million, retiring President Wesley Posvar of the University of Pittsburgh apparently gave back a part of his retirement benefits. A story in the November 25, 1992, issue of the *Chronicle of Higher Education* reported that retiring President David Gardner of the University of California received "a severance package worth $1 million—in a year in which the university's budget was cut by $235 million. The university also announced that 4,000 employees would be cut and that student fees would rise for the third straight year—for a three year total of 85%" (Weiner, 1992, p. B3). The author concludes, "At a time when tuition is going up and universities are viewed by some critics as greedy and unconcerned about educating students, university money must be used for ends more beneficial than lavish executive compensation" (1992, p. B4).

The October 27, 1993, issue of the *Chronicle* carried the story of a $100,000 bonus for University of Oklahoma president Richard L. Van Horn if he stayed in office for at least five years. According to the *Chronicle* story, "Mr. Van Horn, however, thought offering similar bait to his successor would be a bad idea. He says he's been criticized for it since arriving" ("Richard L. Van Horn . . . ," 1993, p. A17). Presumably, Mr. Van Horn will accept the bonus. Would he recommend this form of incentive "bait" for faculty if they remain beyond five years?

As a matter of curiosity, I browsed through issues of the *Chronicle of Higher Education* for a six-month period in the latter part of 1992, looking especially at the personal and professional column carried inside the front page.

• The June 10, 1992, issue carried the story of an assistant dean of students who was arrested on charges of secretly videotaping a female student while she undressed in his apartment ("Stanford University Dean Resigns . . . ," 1992).

• The June 24, 1992, issue carried this headline on page 25: "5 Community College Leaders Indicted in Ohio Contributions Scandal" (Mercer, 1992).

• The August 5, 1992, issue reported that a former director of graduate studies at an East Coast institution had pleaded guilty to stealing more than $300,000 in financial aid funds and extorting money from foreign graduate students attending the institution ("Administrator Stole . . . ," 1992).

• The September 2, 1992, issue reported that the president of a community college had "resigned amid charges that he feigned illness to avoid testifying before the county legislature" ("President Resigns . . . ," 1992). The story goes on to tell that this president was actually attending a conference in another state, giving as an excuse that "his doctor had told him to stay away from stressful situations, and he said that attending the University of Nebraska meeting was less stressful than testifying before the legislature." Who can doubt it?

• The November 11, 1992, issue reported that the budget director for a West Coast university had been reprimanded for performing in a commercial video that portrayed sex between gay men ("Official Is Reprimanded . . . ," 1992).

• The November 25, 1992, issue reported that the board of a northern state technical college had fired the campus president following a state audit that revealed inflated enrollment figures ("Board Fires President . . . ," 1992). This fired president was paid $180,000 for a year and a half of her contract.

• The December 2, 1992, issue reported that a former accountant of a southern university had been indicted on charges of embezzling more than $170,000 from the university's foundation ("Ex-Administrator Indicted . . . ," 1992).

In revisiting the *Chronicle* in recent months, it is disappointing to see that one can continue to find too many similar examples.

Beyond these notable and national instances of collegiate presidential passage and leadership liability, one may consider less spectacular but equally disappointing examples of leadership behavior in higher education. There is the vice president who, in a weekly staff meeting, refers to one of his deans as the south end of a north-bound donkey (using the more efficient three-letter descriptive epithet) and then wonders why this dean is not on his team the next day. Even if one agreed with the vice president's performance/personality assessment of the dean, surely in contemporary leadership volumes there exists guidance that might have helped him find a more helpful approach in communicating his assessment.

Meanwhile, the number of book-length critiques of American higher education rivals the number of volumes on leadership. I can hardly finish reading one book before another appears. There are Cahn's *Saints and Scamps* (1986), Bloom's *The Closing of the American Mind* (1987), Sykes's *Profscam* (1988), Smith's *Killing the Spirit* (1990), D'Souza's *Illiberal Education* (1991), and Anderson's *Impostors in the Temple* (1992). Even more recently, three additional critical volumes have been announced: *How Professors Play the Cat Guarding the Cream* (Huber, 1992), *Up the University: Recreating Higher Education in America* (Solomon and Solomon, 1993), and *The Fall of the Ivory Tower* (Roche, 1993). By the time this manuscript reaches publication, there will no doubt be others.

Lest we believe that the neglect of leadership ideals is peculiar to collegiate America, we would have to look no further than any morning newspaper for stories of criminal misconduct in defense contracting, the investment and financial services business, manufacturing and product safety, pharmaceutical industry, and real estate. Those interested in the written record will find a 1972 volume entitled *In the Name of Profit* (Heilbroner and others) and the more recent 1991 volume by Stewart entitled *Den of Thieves* to be sobering disillusioning reading.

No one would argue that these critiques reflect the dominant reality of corporate or collegiate America. However, one departure from the path of integrity diminishes public trust. For higher education, the evidence is reflected in the number of national conferences devoted to the theme of public trust and to a "loss of sanctuary." Such expository salvos hardly leave the image of higher education unmarked. Is higher education a house where honor dwells? Or is it a place now more ruled by self-interest rather than ideals, a place where the pursuit of power, pay, prestige, and self-interest has estranged both faculty members and administrators from their servant roles. Is higher education more accurately reflected in Galbraith's 1989 novel, *A Tenured Professor,* than in James Hilton's 1934 *Good-Bye, Mr. Chips?*

The preparation of educational leaders is more than a matter of mind and theory. Robert Hutchins once remarked that the chief test of the administrator was more of character than of intellect. I am not sure how sanguine we should be about the extent to which we can shape character at the graduate level. There are, however, empirical and philosophical bases supporting the power of ideals in leadership development and effectiveness. That ideals and values should be a topic of prominent discussion in exercises devoted to leadership development is not at issue. Exploring those ideals and values will constitute a primary engagement of this book.

In examining these topics, current books on leadership are certainly helpful. In addition to the volumes cited in the Preface, Kouzes and Posner's *The Leadership Challenge* (1987), Bolman and Deal's *Reframing Organizations* (1991), and Birnbaum's *How Academic Leadership Works* (1992) offer useful research background, philosophic reflection, and integration of ideas for leaders on the firing line.

While these volumes are worthy contributions to the field, there is still a need to capture the interaction of passion and principle, of ethics and effectiveness. Why do some college administrators not stand for anything? Why do we have a growing literature on leadership and still experience so many disappointing exhibitions of collegiate leaders going astray? As a friend holding an executive appointment in higher education recently queried me, "Why do smart people behave in dumb ways?"

Any collegiate leader can be placed in a climate where conditions of content and context, of people and politics, of finance and fashion, can confine and confuse. Too often, however, college leaders are architects of their own demise. In disappointing displays of ignorance, irresponsibility, and insensitivity, they take themselves, their institutions, and their clients in harm's way. The causes of

performance ineffectiveness are many and will always be complicated combinations of person, position, and context. I believe,
however that many of these disappointing performance records may
be traced to

- A flawed sense of role—a condition of empty vision
- A contempt for ideas—a condition of empty mind
- A neglect of constructive values—a condition of empty heart
- A retreat from servant ideals—a condition of empty spirit
- A violation of cultural norms—a condition of empty sensitivity
- A sacrifice of honor—a condition of empty character

A moderate consideration given to the design of leadership climates can help collegiate leaders avoid these performance pitfalls.

In the context of this discussion, we might note that the
Center for Creative Leadership in Greensboro, North Carolina, has
undertaken several studies of management derailment, where *derailment* is defined as an involuntary and punitive interruption in career after the expectations for a manager are not realized and he or
she is "fired, demoted, or plateaued below expected levels of
achievement" (Lombardo and McCauley, 1988, p. 1). Among the
factors associated with derailment are "problems with interpersonal
relationships, difficulty in molding a staff, and strategic differences
with management" (Lombardo and McCauley, 1988, p. 3). Hidden
in these scholarly descriptors, we could no doubt find the story of
a corporate vice president who, like his collegiate counterpart,
called one of his directors an ass. A few such misadventures in
leadership etiquette will almost certainly lead to "problems with
interpersonal relationships and difficulty in molding staffs."
Strangely missing from the research cited by the Center for Creative
Leadership is any mention of those leaders who derailed their careers because they abandoned their integrity.

As earlier noted, we should not believe that the aberrant leadership behaviors described here and in other records constitute the
only reality—or the dominant reality—in the administration of corporate or collegiate America. There is a reality of goodness—a majority reality—represented in quiet stories of leadership throughout
our nation.

In contrast, I remember Dr. Jerry Boone, now retired vice president for academic affairs of Memphis State University. Upon discovering that one of his more flamboyant department chairs had taken some department faculty members off to a retreat in New Orleans at state expense, Dr. Boone bothered not with the complicated processes of committees and hearings. He used the simple expedient of a phone call to the offending chairman at his hotel in New Orleans. With a tact that even the Mafia might have admired, Jerry invited the chairman to return forthwith and to have in the treasurer's office the next morning a check to cover any and all state monies expended. Here to my personal knowledge was a loving and compassionate man whose caring touch was known to many in the university. But here was a man also properly impatient with nonsense and wrongdoing. Jerry practiced what Thomas Sergiovanni refers to as "leadership by outrage," a concept to which I will return in Chapter Five (1992, p. 130).

How can we hope to prepare the leadership for every sector of our nation without, as Kouzes and Posner suggest in their book *The Leadership Challenge* (1988), "modeling the way" in our own work? Higher education should be a house where honor dwells.

Leader as Designer

Among the more informing and stimulating of current volumes on leadership is Peter Senge's book *The Fifth Discipline*. In its closing pages is an interesting conceptual excursion on "the leader's new work." In a chapter by this title, Senge presents three perspectives of leadership role: the leader as designer, steward, and teacher. The first of these, the concept of design, offers a highly promising way of thinking about leadership. Senge suggests that "design is, by its nature, an integrative science because design requires making something work in practice" (1990, p. 342). I like this thought but would substitute the word *art* for *science*.

Writing in his 1991 book, *Managing as a Performing Art*, Peter Vaill cites particularity, variety, and contextuality as factors that discourage the idea that management and leadership can be viewed only as a science: "The manager cannot choose to banish from the system elements for which there is no adequate science, or if such an attempt is made, the banished elements merely lie dormant until the efforts to keep them out of the system cease; then they flow back in. Thus, the manager's situation is much more like the problem faced by a movie producer, an orchestral conductor, or a director of a play than a scientist" (pp. 121–122). Though complicated enough, the laboratory of the scientist is relatively tame compared to the complexity of the human laboratory that is the university or any other organization. The art form of leadership design therefore constitutes the business of identifying the governing ideals that will give form and foundation to leadership practice.

In a work now almost a half-century old, *The Works of the Mind*, Robert Hutchins remarks "The last question that will be raised about a prospective administrator is whether he has any ideas. If it appears that he has, he is unlikely to be appointed, for he will rightly be regarded as a dangerous man" (1947, p. 150).

We need more dangerous men and women in collegiate leadership ranks today. Men and women who have ideals in head and heart, who use these ideals to design climates for more effective work. While there may be no leadership theory of sufficient embrace to cover the variety of design challenges faced by contemporary collegiate or corporate leaders, there is a cluster of theories that can offer helpful guidance to the curious educational executive.

There are, for example, theories of role that help us think about what leaders are supposed to do. Every leader carries a theory of role across the threshold of his or her office door every day, from the first day of appointment. A theory of role engages that simple but fundamental question, "What am I supposed to do?" and constitutes a beginning point of design. How many collegiate leaders enter their appointment, as we earlier noted, with a flawed vision of role? There are academic cheerleaders, looking for the parade so that they can get in front. There are status fondlers worrying only about the appearance of their calling card. There are information wizards inundated with computer reports and electronic mail addresses. There are educational firemen occupied with crises of their own making. There are trivia worshipers checking forms in stock and occupying their time and energy with the minutia of their unit or campus, enamored of technique but devoid of vision. There are academic mannequins veneered in status but empty of passion and caring. And there are leadership amateurs attempting to guide a precious enterprise with fluffy and empty notions about the content of their work.

The college president who, during his first week in office, directed that a handicapped-student parking place in the administration building lot be painted over so that he could have a reserved space was not thinking deeply about leadership by design. In acquiring his Ph.D, this president had furnished his cerebral chambers with ideas of great complexity, but he apparently had neglected to furnish his heart. In the cerebral chambers, apparently there lodged no theory of leadership role; or else there was deposited there, as we earlier noted, a seriously flawed one.

We are not without good ideas on leadership. Theories of role reveal leadership as a visioning art. Theories of task (making decisions, motivating, managing change and conflict, using power and authority, and so forth) reveal leadership as a conceptual art. Theories of style show that leadership is a performing art. Cultural theories demonstrate leadership as a perceptual art. Theories of value reveal leadership as a moral art. And effectiveness theories show that leadership is an integrating art. The power of an art form will not unfold in the hands of one who is ignorant of the tools involved. "Ignorant artist" is an oxymoron.

What we know will always be a slave to what we believe. "It is not facts, but our beliefs about facts which control our actions," says John Wharton in his essay "Does Anyone Know Reality?" (1966, p. 313). Thus, leadership is a value-based enterprise, and it is here that the most critical design work must take place. A few years ago, while I was chancellor at LSU Shreveport, I managed to discipline myself to early-morning writing time and gave birth to a small book entitled *The Enemies of Leadership* (1985), whose theme was that more managerial malpractice flowed from ill-conceived value dispositions than from technical incompetence:

> In what forum will we learn to revere the dignity and diversity of human personality and to affirm the power and potential of our own personality? What book will teach us to absorb the hostility of the ill informed and the ill mannered but distinguish that

hostility from those who express their loyalty in honest dissent? What seminar will encourage us to let neither dissent nor defeat deny us the power of optimistic spirit? What lesson will require us to probe the limits of our integrity in lonely moments of decision, to find the renewing power that comes to those who exhibit both the courage and the compassion to expect the best of themselves and their colleagues? Where is the examination that will test our inclination to daring rather than to imitation? [p. 3].

The most important design work therefore rests in those governing ideals that guide the minds and hearts of leaders, that establish the form of their characters. There are design ideals whose power and effectiveness can be demonstrated both empirically and philosophically. There are also design ideals that assist in the construction of more effective leadership realities.

The Construction of Leadership Realities

Do leadership ideals help to build leadership realities? In our educational journeys, we learn that truth can be revealed, discovered, and created. In the late fifties, when I was an undergraduate struggling to understand the mysteries of atomic and nuclear physics, our notion of atomic reality was, in retrospect at least, relatively simple. In a planetary analogy, the atom was composed of electrons in energy orbits around the nucleus. The nucleus was composed of protons and neutrons. The Bohr model of atomic structure was elegant, empirically and mathematically satisfying, yielding neat spectroscopic experiments in which the energy levels of the electron structure gave rise to the spectroscopic "fingerprints" marking the special properties of each element.

I learned enough physics to be dangerous. I still enjoy browsing current scientific thought in physics as an intellectual pastime. In recent years, I have found my way through Gary Zukav's *The Dancing Wu Li Masters* (1979), Stephen Hawking's *A Brief History of Time* (1988), Richard Morris's *The Edges of Science* (1991), and Paul Davies's *God and the New Physics* (1983). These books fill me

with a lovely sense of wonder and awe. They also give me a head-
ache. My earlier understanding of atomic reality has fallen apart.
There are now a host of replacement atomic entities, leptons and
hadrons. And these hadrons are composed of quarks, strange and
charmed fellows with spins and up-and-down orientation. And I
now find a host of mind-bending questions that leave me wonder-
ing about this business of reality. Will time someday reverse its path
so that effects precede causes? Is there a dark matter in the universe
whose presence we infer but not yet discern? Are there other "uni-
verses" beyond the one we can sense, and do we create those with
our measurements? These are profound questions, revealing that
the hallway between science and religion may be shorter than we
thought.

But the most mind-boggling dimension of modern physics is
that the nature of reality may not be discerned apart from the observer. Reality is triggered by observation. What and how we elect
to measure may indeed influence reality. Paul Davies poses this
question: "Surely the world out there really exists whether we observe it or not? Surely everything that happens does so for its own
reasons and not because it is being watched? Our observations
might uncover the atomic reality, but how can they create it?" (1983,
p. 103).

Like truth, is reality revealed, discovered, or created? Whether
one is engaged with cosmology or theology, the answers are complex, but it appears that the answer may be that truth is derived
from all three.

In *Leadership and the New Science,* Margaret Wheatley
(1992) offers this provocative note: "I believe in my bones that the
movement towards participation [in management] is rooted, perhaps subconsciously for now, in our changing perceptions of the
universe. This may sound grandiose, but the quantum realm speaks
emphatically to the role of participation, even to its impact on
creating reality" (p. 143). My reading a little physics now and then
is perhaps not such a bad intellectual connection.

Is there a social-behavioral equivalence to the construction of
reality? Certainly, anyone who begins with George Bernard Shaw's
play *Pygmalion,* follows its translation into the Lerner and Lowe
musical *My Fair Lady,* and then reads Rosenthal's "The Pygmalion

Effect Lives" (1973) and Livingston's "Pygmalion in Management" (1969) knows from art and science about how human expectations can influence behavior.

In the field of organizational behavior, one of the more informing and helpful contemporary books is Bolman and Deal's *Reframing Organizations* (1991), in which we learn to "see" the multiple realities of organizations through four different frames of reference. Organizations are *structural* in that they are defined by goals, purpose, mission, and the structural arrangements designed to achieve these. Organizations are composed of *human resources,* men and women whose needs, interests, and motivations add a dimension of complexity to the rational business of pursuing goals. Organizations are *political* because there are always conflicts to be negotiated in the allocation of resources and in the resolution of competing interests. Organizations are *symbolic,* clusters of cultural assumptions and artifacts where appearance can be as important as substance, where the "theater" of organizational life can support or detract from the rational component.

Writing in *Leadership Is an Art,* Max Depree suggests that "the first responsibility of a leader is to define reality. The last is to say thank you" (1989, p. 9). This has to be one of the more concise theories of leadership role to be found in contemporary literature and perhaps one of the best. Is any behavioral principle more firmly established in both empirical and philosophical literature than this: the quality of our expectations is a key determinant in the quality of behavior we elicit from our colleagues and clients? Whether one reads the philosophy of Goethe or the psychology of Rosenthal, it is clear that the value dispositions we carry to our relationships with others are, in part at least, a major factor in defining and designing the reality of those relationships.

Of Principles and Prejudices

The leader's values and ideals contribute, then, to the construction of social reality. Leadership is not a reductionist activity, where we learn to analyze and take problems apart. It is a moral art form as well, a holistic and integrating venture where we make meaning from puzzle pieces. As the *Brothers Karamozov* is more than a collection of words whose grammar and syntax will yield to analysis, leadership is more than its conceptual, skill, and ideological components. That leadership is a moral art form has been asserted by more than one contemporary writer. In *Educational Leadership*, Hodgkinson argues that "in the realm of morals it is not enough to proceed backwards into the future, forever seeking to remedy the ill effects of our actions after the event" (1991, p. 50). The most fundamental act of those who lead is decision making. Decision making implies choice. Choice involves both value and theory, a vision of how things work and how they should work, a mental map representing our vision of social reality: "In the whirl of everyday practice, the direct presence of theory may not be felt. It may indeed be considered irrelevant or, worse, counter-functional. But, despite all denials, it is there. Implicit or tacit, theory always underlies the behavior and actions of the leader. . . . It is the highest function of the executive to develop a deep understanding of self and of his colleagues. . . . the deadliest weapons in the administrative armory are philosophical skills" (Hodgkinson, 1991, p. 112).

Writing in "The Moral Aspect of Leadership" in *On Leadership*, John Gardner observes, "Ultimately we judge our leaders in a framework of values" (1990, p. 67). His framework of values includes that of "high expectations of others," which we have already cited. In a work entitled *Leadership and the Quest for Integrity* (1989), Joseph L. Badaracco, Jr., and Richard Ellsworth have put the term *prejudice* to unexpected usage. They contrast political and directive theories of leadership to those in which leaders are expected to approach the decisions and dilemmas of their role with certain value prejudices—that is, a predisposition to act on particular values. Among those values is a high positive regard for others, another affirmation of a point earlier made.

Nor is this concept of leadership as a moral art form strange to other well-regarded writers. In his widely read book, *Leadership*, James MacGregor Burns notes, "Transforming leadership ultimately becomes moral in that it raises the level of human conduct and ethical aspirations of both leader and led, and thus it has a transforming effect on both. . . . Transcending leadership is dynamic leadership in the sense that leaders throw themselves into a relationship with followers, who will feel 'elevated' by it and often become more active themselves, thereby creating new cadres of leaders" (1978, pp. 4-20).

Additional citations would only cause our attention to wander and our eyes to glaze over. However, let me at least mention several other works that advance leadership as a moral art form: Peter Koestenbaum's *Leadership: The Inner Side of Greatness* (1991), Stephen Covey's *Principle Centered Leadership* (1990), and Thomas Sergiovanni's *Moral Leadership* (1992).

In further illustration of the importance of this topic to collegiate leadership, let us look at Robert Birnbaum's instructive leadership study as described in his 1992 book, *How Academic Leadership Works*. In a concluding chapter entitled "Lessons for Successful Leadership," Birnbaum advises leaders to "emphasize strong values." Leadership is ultimately a moral act because it involves interpretations of what an institution should do. Effective presidents act with a moral foundation that permits them to retain their equilibrium even as they are being buffeted by events (Birnbaum, 1992).

The Center of Mind and Heart

The renowned philosopher of science René Dubos once noted that "human institutions must be held together by forces of a spiritual nature" (1981, p. 133), an insightful way of thinking about leadership. Who will follow those that have no center of mind and heart? The most urgent business for the collegiate leader, or any leader, is the construction of philosophy. In the chapters to follow, my hope is to highlight those ideals that are most likely to yield effective leadership behavior, that furnish constructive and positive vehicles for putting knowledge to work, that fashion and channel leadership skill, that constitute a leadership philosophy.

In the modest collection of books on leadership in my office, I can count perhaps a hundred volumes. I can count on one hand, however, the number of those where the word *honor* is found in the table of contents or index. A premier design ideal of effective leadership is that of honor. Honor is first a vision of what constitutes right action. More importantly, honor involves the will to act on the basis of that vision. It is a first principle, a first ideal of leadership by design.

2

The Dignity Test

A moment in my former life as chancellor at LSU Shreveport is etched clearly in memory. One morning as I labored away with papers on my desk, a very large man suddenly appeared in my office. His weight I would estimate at three hundred pounds, and his arms were about the size of my legs. The most important sensory intelligence, however, was that he was not smiling. I immediately concluded that the work on my desk was trivial and rose to shake his hand, asking if I could help him. Here is his story.

It seems that this thirty-year-old student had enrolled in one of our evening courses for the fall term, making this investment in learning while driving a truck during the day. Believing that he might have made at least a C in the course, he was both surprised and disappointed to receive a grade of F. He dutifully made an appointment to visit with the professor, who kept him waiting for thirty minutes while she had coffee with colleagues. When the student was finally admitted, the professor admitted that she could not find his final examination and that she would have to think about whether this warranted corrective action on her part.

The student did not consult the student handbook and the grievance process contained therein. Nor did he consult the department chair, dean, or provost. With malice in his heart, he computed the most direct path to my office, where my diminutive secretary

understandably concluded that the size of the issue and the suppli-
cant justified an interruption to the routine of the morning.

At LSU Shreveport, we had managed over a period of years
to insert values commitments into our mission statement. One of
these read as follows: "We will treat our students and our colleagues
with dignity, rendering instructional and administrative service
marked by courtesy and competence." This statement constituted a
salutary behavior and performance standard for everyone in the
university. I referred to it as the "dignity test. Here appeared to be
an instance where we had fallen short of our code.

I placed phone calls to the appropriate chairman, dean, and
the provost and asked if they might come to my office for a brief
visit, where I had the student repeat his story. Promising him a
follow-up, I remained in conversation with these three academic
administrators, asking if they thought we had met the dignity test
in this situation. A consensus was not difficult to achieve, after
which I invited the three to see what resolution might be found for
this issue.

Let me be quick to note that this situation was a rare departure in the behavior of our faculty and staff during the ten years of
my tenure as chancellor at that institution. The faculty had earned
a splendid reputation for caring and competence, and we had performance data on a number of public measures to complement the
reputation. I rarely appeared anywhere in the city without receiving
compliments on the devotion and teaching skill of our faculty, and
I tried to pass each of those compliments along to the faculty in
personal visits, calls, and notes. This reputation for outstanding
teaching had been earned over many years—a fact that, in my mind,
made it all the more imperative to deal thoughtfully with this apparent departure.

Now back to the story. The offending faculty member had an
unfortunate history of such cavalier treatment of students and is no
longer on the faculty at LSU Shreveport. The student in question
walked across the stage at my final commencement in December of
1990 to receive his bachelor's degree and to give me a smile and a
handshake that was, to my relief, happily firm and less punishing
than his musculature might have produced. I hope that he will be
a happy and capable ambassador for the university.

A line attributed to American gangster Al Capone goes something like this: "You can get much farther with a kind word and a gun than you can with a kind word alone." This, however, is not a useful or recommended tactic for collegiate leaders. A modified version is that you can go much farther with a kind word and a commitment to basic values—of which dignity is a premier example—than you can with a kind word alone.

A Value Legacy

If I were to distill all of the principles and advice that can be found in this and a hundred other books on leadership and leave only one word with those who aspired to leadership, I would want that conceptual and value legacy to be conveyed by *dignity,* or simply treating others with respect. Dignity must be considered, as I have already noted, a powerful and constructive performance standard. The importance of the dignity principle is affirmed in both philosophical and empirical literature and also within our daily experience.

In his 1965 treatise, *Eupsychian Management,* psychologist Abraham Maslow offers this reflection. After examining the tendency to consider humans as interchangeable parts in our organizations, Maslow says, "Then I think also that this kind of psychodynamic understanding of self-esteem and of dignity would make a great difference in the industrial situation because the feelings of dignity, of respect and of self-respect are so easy to give! It costs little or nothing, it's a matter of an attitude, a deep-lying sympathy and understanding which can express itself almost automatically in various ways that can be quite satisfying, since they save the dignity of the person in the unfortunate situation" (1965, p. 48). Why, if it costs little or nothing, do we see so many leaders violating this simple value? I am still struggling with the answer to that question.

Dignity is advanced if one thinks about the power of the reciprocity principle: would I want done to me what I am about to do to another? And we would assume that reasonably smart folks might have been exposed to the power of the reciprocity principle at some point in their educational lives. William Hitt of the Battelle

Institute reveals in *The Leader Manager* (1988) that the reciprocity principle is celebrated in every great religious literature of the world:

> Buddhism—Hurt not others with that which pains
>   yourself.
> Christianity—Therefore all things whatsoever ye
>   would that men should do to you, do ye even so to
>   them.
> Confucianism—What you do not want done to your-
>   self do not do unto others.
> Hinduism—Good people proceed while considering
>   what is best for others is best for themselves.
> Islam—No one of you is a believer until he loves for
>   his brother what he loves for himself.
> Judaism—And thy shalt love thy neighbor as thyself.
> Zoroastrianism—Whatever is disagreeable to yourself
>   do not do unto others [p. 173].

A mystery of history and human behavior is how we have such a bloody record of religious wars and how we experience so much ideological conflict within and between each of these religious-thought systems when dignity and reciprocity are their foundation principles. How difficult it is to honor in our behavior the values we profess individually and collectively.

Another incentive for treating colleagues and others within the circle of our influence with dignity is that we invite retribution if we do not. Many motives for human behavior are built on elements of both nobility and self-interest. Thus, there is a noble reason for treating our colleagues with dignity: because the exercise of this design ideal respects their personality and honors the reciprocity principle. If that is not a sufficient reason, however, it does not hurt to remember that the failure to do so invites an "eye for an eye" response; by doing harm to another, we invite harm to ourselves. Unhappy—and unnecessary—surprises may await the leader who surrenders courtesy and civility in favor of harshness and arrogance, who does not know how to practice "civil rites."

In the dusty shelves of my memory is the vague remembrance

of lines from Emerson, which I reproduce here in their full form:
"Things refuse to be mismanaged long. Though no checks to a new
evil appear, the checks exist, and will appear. . . . Every secret is
told, every crime is punished, every virtue rewarded, every wrong
redressed, in silence and certainty" (1929, pp. 155–156).

In *On Leadership,* John Gardner says that one of the goals
of moral leadership is the "release of human potential" (1990, p.
73). We can hardly expect to accomplish that goal if we fail to treat
our colleagues and our students with dignity, if we do not discover
within our leadership intent and style the language and behavior
of affirmation.

Let me move now to reflections designed to bring additional
operational clarity to the meaning of dignity in collegiate settings.

Performance Rather Than Pedigree

In 1969, Dr. C. C. "Sonny" Humphreys, the president of Memphis
State University, asked if I would be willing to move from my five-
year appointment as director of records–registrar for the university
to appointment as director of institutional research. This was an
opportunity to gain new knowledge and perspective and to experience new challenge, so I accepted readily.

Already at work in the office was a young man named Jerry
Matthews. I perceived that Jerry had three notable problems. First,
he did not wear a tie to work. Some of my friends harbor suspicions
that I sleep in a tie. Nevertheless, I was a bit worried about this
careless attitude toward appearance and office decorum. Adding to
this "problem" was Jerry's beard. The beard suggested other careless personal tendencies, according to my view of reality. Even so,
I might have overlooked these two matters had it not been for Jerry's
third "problem." In his office right next to mine, he kept a pet boa
constrictor in a large glass tank, which also contained two mice, one
black and one white. Every two weeks, one of the mice would disappear, with a long delayed resolution of its anxiety. The cleaning
crew would not touch Jerry's office, which added further disarray.

Thus, Jerry started out as a potential and unknowing victim
of my prejudices. Soon, however, I learned an important lesson
about Jerry Matthews and about prejudice. Jerry could make our

IBM mainframe computer stand on its head and turn flips. His software gymnastics made it possible for us to develop rapidly new information systems for student enrollment management, facilities management, and financial aid management. And we were one of the first institutions in the state to complete a newly inaugurated cost study that had been initiated by the Tennessee Higher Education Commission. Once I learned this information about Jerry, he could have come to the office in his underwear, had a beard that reached to the floor, and kept a pet tiger in his office. It turned out, of course, that Jerry's problems were really not his but mine. We were an odd but effective pair. My button-down oxford shirt, regimental tie, and tassel loafers were able to team up with his denim shirt, blue jeans, and sandals in a manner that might not have been predicted by conventional wisdom.

Fortunately, the ideal of dignity had guided me, and I had kept my prejudices privately contained in initial interactions with Jerry; I thus had time to concentrate on performance. But how often do we make prisoners of our colleagues with our prejudgments? And is there any organized enterprise more rife with such prejudices than colleges and universities? I have lost track of Jerry over the years, but it would not surprise me to learn that he was president of his own software company. Perhaps he was using some of that software to manage his considerable investment portfolio, while his pet boa constrictor considered the availability of a half-dozen mice instead of two.

I reviewed the job description for the presidency of a research university recently. Among the desirable qualifications confected by members of the search committee were these: the "new president should be a distinguished scholar in one of the traditional arts or sciences. . . . A respected professional, one possessing 'charisma.'" Dull folks from engineering, law, education, agriculture, and other disciplines might think before applying to this search, or at least ask where they might find some charisma. In another presidential search for a land-grant university, the search committee developed the collected opinion that a candidate who had not served in a land-grant university would be ill equipped to handle the leadership challenges of that university. Several able candidates were jettisoned as a result of the screening test. And in a third presidential search, a dean on the search committee remarked that one of the finalists did not have the stature for leadership. Somewhere along the way to his Ph.D., this dean had arrived at the conclusion that presidents performed more effectively if they were six feet or above. Concentrating on pedigree rather than performance, a private research university placed in the president's office a nationally recognized Ph.D. in science, only to discover in a few months that his leadership skills were still very much in the embryo stage. His short tenure of two years contributed to the turnover statistics we cited in Chapter One.

The leader who hopes to treat colleagues and clients with dignity will look for the performance promise and will evaluate the record of colleagues rather than confine them with unfortunate and unexamined prejudices of process and pedigree.

Improvement Rather Than Punishment

Years ago, I taught an early-morning class. Enrolled in this 7:00 A.M. class was a young man from Brooklyn, New York, that I shall refer to as "Matt." Matt was not a student that I might describe as unusually brilliant in the academic and conventional sense of that term. When he turned in a paper that looked as though he had been using Bill Buckley's dictionary, it was natural for me to entertain a suspicion as to whether Matt had done the work.

Now as all good teachers know, when you suspect students of cheating, it may be unwise to accuse them outright. A more oblique tactic may commend itself. And so I invited Matt over to have a cup of hot chocolate. I said to him, "Matt, what does this word *oxymoron* on page 6 mean?"

He said, "Read me the sentence, Dr. Bogue." And so I did. He replied, "Well, I can't remember exactly what that word means."

I then asked, "Well, what does this word *autochthonous* on page 11 mean?"

He again responded, "Read me the sentence, Dr. Bogue," which I did, with the same blank response as before.

Finally, I inquired, "Well, let me try one more time. What does the word *pusillanimous* on page 15 mean?"

By this point in our exchange, Matt was, as we say in the

South, grinning like a mule eating briars. And so I asked, "Matt, did you write this paper?"

With a knowing grin breaking on his face, he said, "No."

"Who wrote this paper, Matt?" I inquired.

"My girlfriend," he replied.

I noted that I thought I might give her an A but that we needed some serious talk about what grade Matt was going to get. I then invited him to take his person out of the office and to bring me a paper within a week that he had written. He did. Today, Matt is doing something that I am not smart enough or talented to do. He is teaching mentally and emotionally retarded children, bringing independence to their lives—a fine test of performance on the part of any teacher.

A note in passing. Leaders do well to consider the power of questions in the negotiation of human relations. A well-constructed question will often carry as much power in a softer delivery than a sharply worded accusation or reprimand. Working in the interrogatory mood can often be more effective than the imperative mood when it comes to the evaluation of human performance.

If we want to treat others with dignity, we look first to improving performance rather than meting out punishment. And we are more patient with mistakes. A vice president for one of our larger corporations made a large-scale error in judgment related to the design and manufacture of a new company product. The decision resulted in a seven-figure loss. When summoned to the president's office, the vice president fully expected to be fired. Yet the president was of another opinion; he remarked that the company had too much invested in what the vice president might have learned from his error in judgment and that this person should convert this dearly purchased leadership wisdom into a more profitable venture for the company.

Responsibility Rather Than Dependence

The old word is *trust*. The new word is *empowerment*. Both mean that we invest our colleagues with the opportunity to stretch their talents to the far reach of their abilities. Bestowing responsibility should be accompanied, however, by holding colleagues responsible.

A little-known story found in a little-known book released by a little-known publisher is *"You Dropped It, You Pick It Up,"* written by Jim Paul (1983) and published by Ed's Publishing Company in Baton Rouge, Louisiana. This is a story about a football team from a Tennessee college.

In the fall of 1916, a "pick up" football team from Cumberland University in Lebanon, Tennessee, traveled to Atlanta to play a game contracted with the Georgia Tech football team coached by the famed John Heisman. The extent to which the gentlemen from Tennessee were outclassed is reflected in the final score: Georgia Tech 222, Cumberland 0. Now this game and score must occupy a record in someone's book of bizarre sporting events. It was a game in which two Cumberland players went AWOL, hiding outside the field until the contest was over; one in which another Cumberland player was found hiding on the Georgia Tech bench so that he could avoid being inserted into a humiliating and bruising encounter with the larger Georgia Tech players; a game in which Coach Allen from Cumberland took part in the last play.

The play from which the book draws its title, however, occurred late in the game and is reported as follows:

> The next play called for Johnny Dog to run around
> left end. After receiving the snap, Johnny headed left;
> but, unable to get a good grip on the ball, he fumbled
> it. Slowly it rolled toward George Allen, stopping by
> his right foot.
> "Pick it up, fullback!" Johnny Dog yelled.
> Jumping away from the ball, afraid of getting
> crushed by the huge Tech linemen closing in on them,
> Allen yelled back,"You dropped it, you pick it up!"
> [pp. 217–218].

"You dropped it, you pick it up." There is much to commend this advice in our daily leadership ventures. The advice commends the idea of responsibility—that is, that our colleagues attend to the responsibility of their roles and positions, make the required decisions, and take the consequences of these.

Shortly after assuming the chancellor's position at LSU Shreveport in the summer of 1980, I was approached by a deputation of the newly appointed graduate faculty. These individuals invited me to decide what faculty group would approve graduate courses: the newly appointed graduate faculty council or the old course and curriculum committee. This was a question designed to discover whether the new chancellor harbored the qualities of an academic Solomon. It occurred to me, however, that the inquiry and the responsibility did not belong to me at this point.

I invited the vice chancellor for academic affairs into the discussion and indicated that I intended to hold the vice chancellor responsible for all policy, program, and personnel matters in academic affairs. I asked him to consider the matter further and bring me a recommendation. And he did, with a proposal that acknowledged the changing complexion of the university in the implementation of its new graduate programs and the evolving governance role of various faculty committees.

The more uncomfortable and risky the decision climate, the more eager colleagues will be to pass the pressure to those above and to engage in *High Noon* behavior (from the classic Western movie of that title) by retreating to safe and anonymous places away from perceived dangers. For unhappy salary decisions, for example, there will be some chairmen and deans who would prefer that negatively affected faculty members believe that the "black hat" is worn by the next academic administrator up the line. And even the best of presidents will yearn to pass the buck to the board on occasion. A willingness to stand responsible for one's own duty and the consequences of one's own decisions and an insistence that colleagues do the same is another operational test of whether leaders treat colleagues' clients with dignity.

There are other operational tests of what it means to treat others with dignity. One is the test of candor, and another is the test of quality or excellence. While a fuller treatment on these two design ideals follow in subsequent chapters, let me offer here a brief illustrative note on the relationship between dignity and the ideals of candor and excellence.

A newly appointed president took office as the budget for the new year was being planned, an activity involving the setting of raises. Her vice president for academic affairs came in to discuss his recommendations on raises for five deans and indicated that he planned raises for all deans but one. He then elevated an inquiring eyebrow to the new president, as though he expected some affirming comment.

Having been in office less than one week and knowing little of the performance history of either the vice president or any of the deans, the new president posed these questions. "As for the dean for whom you are not recommending a raise, have you over the past year discussed those matters of performance that have led you to this decision on his salary?" The vice president replied that he had not. A second question followed. "Have you personally visited with the dean concerning your decision not to recommend a raise for him?" The vice president again reported that he had not. The third question was as follows. "Do you intend to visit personally with your dean and advise him that you did not recommend a raise for him?" The vice president answered that the final budget document would communicate that decision to the dean.

The final question was "And is this the way you would like to be treated in our relationship—for any perceived performance liability to remain hidden, to discover the effect of performance judgments only in salary decisions, and to learn of negative assessments and decisions through the impersonal expression of the final budget?" The vice president responded that he would like to think about those questions.

The test of candor is so simple; in this and most cases it marries nicely with the ideal of reciprocity. There are positive dividends in treating colleagues with candor and courtesy. Empirical and philosophical studies support the probability of positive results when we do and also predict high probability of unhappy consequences when we do not. Our experience will often confirm these probabilities. Let me turn now to the relationship between dignity and excellence.

In a recent word-association exercise, I watched a seminar class of organizational executives spend an hour filling a blackboard with their response to the word *management*. Other words

included *power, authority, process, responsibility, decision, budgeting, empowering, vision, mission,* and *evaluation.* Not until an
hour had passed, however, did the word *customer* or *client* enter the
conversation. And the terms *ethics, integrity,* and *dignity* never
appeared.

Consider this news clip appearing in the *San Francisco
Chronicle* on August 25, 1993:

> Why is Wendy Rouder standing there looking
> puzzled? Because she registered at City College by
> phone—a new system—and then mailed in the fees for
> two courses, plus $10 for a campus parking sticker.
> Simple, wot? Not. Back came a receipt but no parking
> sticker. However, it did show a $10 overpayment so all
> is swell? Well: she went out to the school and stood in
> line for an hour to get the parking sticker. "That'll be
> $10," said the bureaucrat, at which Wendy trium-
> phantly presented the credit slip, to no avail. "You'll
> have to give me $10 if you want the sticker now, and
> then you may apply for a refund, which'll take about
> eight weeks," he said, not unkindly. Defeated, Wendy
> asked for a refund form. "Here you go," he said, hand-
> ing her one, "but you won't get any money back.
> There's a $10 fee for processing a refund [Caen, 1993,
> p. 6].

Does this illustration represent excellence of performance in City
College's enrollment system? And did this student get treated with
dignity at City College? Concepts of quality and excellence interact
with the ideal of dignity, and I will have more to say on the theme
of excellence in Chapter Seven. Ensuring that our colleagues and
our clients are treated with dignity thus requires that we attend to
the performance of our systems and policies as well as that of
individuals.

Abandoned to the Gift of Others

During recent months, I have discovered many readings that support the dignity test. An interesting set of ideas and tactics can be

found in *Getting to Yes,* a book about negotiating agreement without giving in (Fisher and Ury, 1981). Recommending that leaders
abandon both hard and soft approaches to bargaining and negotiation in favor of a principled approach, authors Fisher and Ury
propose these ideas: "1. Separate the people from the problem. 2.
Focus on interests, not positions. 3. Invent options for mutual gain.
4. Insist on using objective criteria" (p. 11). In the later pages of
Getting to Yes can be found this advice: "As a negotiator, you will
almost always want to look for solutions that will leave the other
side satisfied as well. If the customer feels cheated in a purchase, the
store owner has also failed; he may lose a customer and his reputation may suffer. An outcome in which the other side gets absolutely nothing is worse for you than one which leaves them
mollified. In almost every case, your satisfaction depends to a degree
on making the other side sufficiently content with an agreement to
want to live up to it" (p. 75).

    Thus, the leader interested in putting the dignity test to work
avoids making enemies out of those with whom he or she disagrees
and shuns unnecessary zero-sum outcomes. Years ago, when I served
as a director of institutional research, a group of angry students
approached me to seek help in developing an instrument that they
intended to use in evaluating teaching at Memphis State University.
The students had become frustrated in trying to persuade the faculty
to develop and adopt both a policy and an instrument, and so they
had decided to operate their own system. Utilizing several of the
just-expressed philosophical and tactical ideas, the provost and I
were able to set in motion a faculty-student task force to examine
the issue; the task force was composed of student leaders and faculty
members enjoying high trust and authority with both students and
their colleagues. The outcome of the task force was a policy and an
instrument that nicely met interests and concerns of both the faculty
and the students. Adversaries became partners.

    In his engaging book *Leadership Is an Art,* Max Depree
offers an insight early on that "understanding and accepting diversity enables us to see that each of us is needed. It also enables us to
think about being abandoned to the strengths of others, of admit-
ting that we cannot know or do everything" (1989, p. 7). What a
lovely turn of phrase—"abandoned to the strengths of others."

A reading and learning venture supporting the beauty and power of the diversity celebrated by Max Depree was my exposure to the Myers-Briggs Type Indicator (MBTI), a personality theory and accompanying diagnostic instrument that allows us to think with greater clarity and sensitivity about personality differences. There are

Two ways of perceiving: sensing and intuiting
Two ways of judging: thinking and feeling
Two ways of expressing interest in the outer world: extraversion and introversion
Two ways of relating to outer world: judging and perceiving

In *Gifts Differing* (1980), Isabel Briggs Myers furnishes an informing conceptual tour of the MBTI. Leaders who have been exposed to this theory of personality differences may well come away with greater sensitivity to and understanding of the gifts of others. The investment of reading time will help leaders appreciate that their way of approaching the world is not the only way or the only reality. The ability to respect differences in personality and perception is fundamental to the effective exercise of the design ideal of dignity.

A third volume that speaks to the theme of diversity and dignity is *Women's Ways of Knowing* by Mary Belenky (1986), a book conceptually indebted to Carol Gilligan's *In a Different Voice: Psychological Theory and Women's Development* (1982). Earlier in the work by Belenky is this arresting line: "At first the insight that each of us looks through a different lens can be profoundly disturbing, because it suggests that each of us is profoundly alone" (p. 97). Yet knowing that others gaze through a different lens may put us in good company and thus moderate our aloneness. It will also help us accord others the dignity of their views and beliefs.

The Empiricism of "Being Nice"

We have built our development in this chapter heavily on personal and philosophical discourse. Is there empirical support for the ideal of dignity? Robert Axelrod's *The Evolution of Cooperation* engages the following question: "When should a person cooperate, and when should a person be selfish, in an ongoing interaction with another person?" (1984, p. vii). A goodly portion of the book is taken with playing a game called the Prisoner's Dilemma. The dilemma is operationally illustrated in Mullen and Roth's (1991) book called *Decision Making:*

> Sue and Harry are caught by the police as they are preparing to rob a jewelry store. The chief immediately separates them. Knowing that his case is weak without a confession, he makes the same offer to each. If one confesses and the other does not, the one who confesses goes free. If both confess, they both get put away for ten years. If one confesses and the other doesn't, then the one who doesn't gets fifteen years hard labor. Each knows that if neither confesses both will get two years on reduced charges [pp. 7–8].

Axelrod reports that the strategy most effective for any party playing this game is also the simplest one, which he labels the "tit for tat" strategy. The assumptions related to the playing of this game are not far from those we encounter in our leadership lives.

How, then, shall we begin the day? Will we assume that life is a chess game in which the other person is out to get us? Or is another more constructive assumption more appropriate? Axelrod believes there is. If both parties are interested in advancing their self-interest, the first move in the Prisoner's Dilemma game is to cooperate and then follow the lead of the other player. If the other player defects while you are cooperating, then your next move is to defect. If the other player cooperates, then you continue to cooperate.

In computer simulations of Prisoner's Dilemma and in actual player participation, "Surprisingly, there is a single property which distinguishes the relatively high-scoring entries from the relatively low-scoring entries. This is the property of being nice, which is to say never being the first to defect" (Axelrod, 1984, p. 33). Axelrod goes on to observe that "even expert strategists from political science, sociology, economics, psychology, and mathematics made the systematic errors of being too competitive for their own good, not being forgiving enough, and being too pessimistic about the responsiveness of the other side" (p. 40).

In Chapter One, we cited the elements of expectancy theory and the empirical work of Rosenthal and Livingston, suggesting that belief affects behavior and that our expectations condition behavior outcomes. Belief may also affect biology! The power of our attitudes has nowhere been demonstrated more powerfully than in health care. And from my vantage point, few spokesmen are more eloquent on this point than a nonphysician, Norman Cousins. Built on experiences and work associated with his appointment to the UCLA Medical School, Cousins furnishes in his book *Head First: The Biology of Hope* (1989) the evidence for how hope, faith, love, purpose, and laughter can help combat serious disease. Though the empirical studies cited in this volume will please the scientists among us, it is the examples and illustrations—the literature of hope and laughter—that compel our attention.

Cousins recites a story of making rounds in the hospital with the dean of the medical school and several residents and interns. Coming upon a wasted patient from a Latin American country sitting in a wheelchair, the dean discovered in his weak exchange with the patient, with confirmation from the ward nurses, that he had not been eating. Additional inquiry elicited the response that the hospital did not offer anything that the patient liked. (It will not surprise any of us that the probability of finding refried beans, beef fajitas, and jalapeño peppers on the hospital menu is about the same as sneaking daybreak past a healthy rooster.)

When the dean queried the residents and interns about the possibility of finding this patient something he would like to eat, they recoiled in disbelief, asking the dean if he thinks they are likely to find suitable "hot stuff" in the hospital kitchen. The dean then asked the residents and interns this question: if this patient needed a medication that the hospital did not carry in its pharmacy, did they think that they would be able to obtain it? No argument there! Well, the patient was given some Mexican food and was discharged in three weeks.

Do leadership values and ideals define reality, as Max Depree has suggested? The simple response is yes. Empirical studies and illustrations from education, business, and health care affirm the validity of this idea. Our attitudes and our values do indeed contribute to our social and behavioral realities.

Everyone a Volunteer: A Summary Note

The dignity test is a compelling and constructive guide for effective leadership behavior, a test regrettably neglected. In revisiting a book in my library the other day, I came across a line that encourages leaders to remember and practice the power of the dignity test. From *The Leadership Challenge* by Kouzes and Posner (1987) comes this challenge: "To get a feel for the true essence of leadership, assume that everyone who works for you is a volunteer" (p. 26).

If we want to stir the subterranean fires that burn within the minds and hearts of our colleagues, if we want to awaken the quiet hopes that reside there, if we want to tap our colleagues' magnificent power of intellect and imagination, if we want to call others to the far reaches of their potential, if we want to discover the strength of devotion and the power of allegiance, then we will evaluate thought and behavior by the standards of the dignity test.

3

The Habit of Curiosity

Academic leaders hold in trust the mission of learning organizations. Colleges and universities embrace in their mission the dissemination, the production, the conservation, the application, and the evaluation of knowledge. This mission assumes the continuing and active exercise of curiosity on the part of both faculty and staff. Can academic leaders expect of others what they are not willing to demonstrate in their own lives?

A touch of wonder, a compulsive curiosity. Is it too much to ask that leaders of learning organizations, of colleges and universities, exhibit and model in their own behavior a habit that we aspire to commend and cultivate in the lives of faculty and students? Learning is freedom's instrument to save mind and heart from the bondage of narrow and limited perspective. The instrument leaps to use, however, only with the impetus of our curiosity.

The Music Within

It would be difficult to select any book on leadership without finding there that leaders are expected to have "vision"—some commanding and convincing idea about where and how collegiate organizations should be moving to the future. There is also dissent on the nature and importance of leadership vision. Whatever our

33

perspective on the nature and nurture of leadership vision, we might be disappointed to encounter a new director, dean, vice president, or president and discover that the rooms of his or her mind were mostly vacant. I remember participating in a planning forum years ago in which a few faculty members were bemoaning the fact that the chair and the dean already had an agenda concerning possible new directions for their departments and college. The discussion eventually and not unexpectedly turned to the question of whether there was any value in the faculty investing time and thought in exploring and designing new directions if the chair and dean already had a plan in mind.

One faculty member asked her assembled colleagues if they would prefer that the chair and dean came to their positions devoid of both ideas and passion? Would not this emptiness be more bothersome than an academic leader who at least has some idea and conviction? Should the faculty assume that the chair and dean had no capacity for learning? Would these two be as likely to learn if the faculty did not offer contrasting design options? And how probable would it be that the faculty and chair or dean would discover the power of multiple intelligence at work if the faculty vacated the discussion, leaving the ideas from the chair and dean as the only ones on the table?

Leader as visionary, leader as learner—are these two roles in conflict? The answer is clearly no. One role is companion to the other. How many of us have begun a journey with a vision in mind, only to discover along the way that a more compelling and satisfying conceptual destination was possible? Only in that delicate negotiation of conviction and compromise can we know the excitement of learning. Conviction is both end and means of learning. It is the result of having taken a learning journey, and it is the stimulus that encourages us to launch a new one.

At the turn of the nineteenth century, the Michelson Morely experiment in physics began with the vision or the intent of proving that light and electromagnetic radiation traveled through an "ether" surrounding the earth. Logically, the experimenters reasoned, if light did travel through this substance, it would move faster when flowing with the ether and slower in the reverse direction, much as a boat traverses the river more swiftly when moving downstream with the current than when fighting it going upstream. In terms of the basic hypothesis and theory undergirding the experiment, it was a notable failure, yet one for which we all may give thanks. The results opened avenues for new ways of thinking about light propagation. This experiment yielded a moment, as Thomas Kuhn suggests, of scientific revolution, necessitating that old models of thought be replaced by a new perspective (1962).

In the now-famous Hawthorne studies, psychologist Elton Mayo and colleagues began their study of the relay assembly room at the Western Electric plant with the idea of showing that worker productivity is positively related to environmental conditions such as level of illumination (Mayo, 1945). As most students of human relations now know, this experiment was also a failure—at least in terms of the hypotheses posed. It also marked the transition in organizational and leadership studies from the themes of efficiency and instrumentation to a concern for the needs and aspirations of those human resources that give life to any organization. The vision of workers as interchangeable parts in the system was rendered obsolete by this social science learning experience.

How many other examples in the field of human inquiry could we cite to show the importance of learning journeys? The salient point is not that these ventures in scientific and social settings have resulted in surprising and helpful conclusions, even when cloaked in error. That many of these learning journeys would never have been undertaken at all had it not been for the stimulative and sustaining force of curiosity is significant.

These opening notes, then, celebrate the leadership ideal of curiosity. Yet we are not only saluting the importance of the leader's cultivating the habit of curiosity but also his or her ability to create community curiosity, to design and energize a learning organization. In *The Fifth Discipline*, Peter Senge (1990) argues that it will not be possible to meet the future with only a grand strategist at the helm, a single individual holding in hand the keys to the future. Nor can the future be met by analytical learning alone, by taking things apart. He argues that the challenge of leadership will be to tap the natural curiosity of each and every person in an organization and to encourage more "systems" thinking (the fifth discipline) so that people discern the interaction of structures, events, and policies.

In *Managing as a Performing Art*, Peter Vaill describes the necessity for a "community of vision and feeling" (1991, p. 111). A community of curiosity, of vision, is a protection against the potential narrowness and arrogance of individual thought, a protection against groupthink.

Writing in the winter 1991 issue of *National Forum*, Suzanne Morse expresses the matter this way: "Our leaders will be called on to lead in a different way. Their job will be to create spaces and opportunities for people to come together—in the community, in business, in religious organizations, in civic groups, and in government—to discover their common interests and decide on courses of action. To paraphrase William James's words, leaders will help us find the music within us to create a different world" (p. 3). The learning leader releases the "music within." Realizing the promise of those entrusted to our care is a primary outcome of leader curiosity.

Two collegiate presidential exemplars come quickly to mind. I think of Charles McClain, former president at Northeast Missouri State University, and Sister Joel Read, president at Alverno College. Both of these individuals invested long years in leading their institutions to the forefront of college outcomes assessment. They encouraged initiatives in assessment long before it became the current popular preoccupation. They created learning communities by involving their faculties and staffs in sustained efforts to define and evaluate learning outcomes and to apply the results in the improvement of both program and student performance. They released the music within. What other factors recommend the power of curiosity?

Modeling the Way

In a previous chapter, we mentioned a leadership role dimension found in the Kouzes and Posner book *The Leadership Challenge* (1987). Among the six role dimensions these two authors factored from their research studies of leaders performing at their best was that of "modeling the way." In the words of Kouzes and Posner,

"Leaders stand up for their beliefs. They practice what they preach. They show others by their own example that they live by the values that they profess. Leaders know that while their position gives them authority, their behaviors earn them respect. It is consistency between words and actions that builds a leader's credibility" (p. 187).

One of the ironic features of this particular section of the Kouzes and Posner book is that Donald Kennedy, former president of Stanford University, was used as an example of a collegiate leader who modeled the way. Citing several illustrations of President Kennedy's style and presence on the campus, Kouzes and Posner conclude that "it is Kennedy's clarity about his values and how he behaves which sends messages about what is and is not important in how the organization operates" (p. 190).

This principle of leading by example can hardly be faulted. In the case of this particular illustration, however, there is a sad postscript. Subsequent stories appearing in the *Chronicle of Higher Education* (Cordes, 1991a, 1991b) report President Kennedy's being put on the congressional griddle for alleged irregularities in federal research grant overhead charges at Stanford. As we saw earlier, Kennedy eventually resigned his presidency because of sustained negative publicity associated with these charges.

As an aside, I have always thought it might be instructive to furnish aspiring collegiate leaders with sample press releases of administrative entries and exits. For some presidents and other academic officers, I suspect that these media reports would show as much contrast as the first and final acts for some football coaches. The entry fanfare for the academic matador can be an exciting and beguiling call. For the academic leader who abandons curiosity and other governing ideals, the exit dirge may mask the memory of the opening fanfare.

The alert and curious academic leader is open to lessons that flow from experiences both welcome and unwelcome and models the ideal of curiosity before his or her colleagues. The curious collegiate leader knows the potentially inhibiting force of anxiety, the retrospective pleasure of adventure, the informing power of action, the reinforcing touch of achievement. No lesson is lost on the learning leader, and each lesson strengthens leader artistry.

Strengthening the Art Form

With good ideas and with practice, the learning leader has an opportunity to strengthen the art form of leadership. In addition to the
extensive general literature and that specific to leadership in collegiate settings, the evolution of research on leadership has given us
efficiency, human relations, style, decision, culture, and quality
models. Yet as previously mentioned, some holding acadmic leadership responsibility have little acquaintance with this literature,
and others disdain the need to do so.

Leadership is an integrative art form that begins with knowledge. Every leader carries multiple theories across the threshold of
his or her office door every day. We all have ideas on how things
do and should work. Whether our knowledge is informed by scholarship in the field of leadership is the important question.

Earlier, I indicated that there were theories of role, task, style,
culture, ethics, and effectiveness—with an informing philosophical
and empirical base underlying each. Without the driving force of
curiosity, however, the power of these theories will not open to us.
In illustration, I want to select one of these theoretical domains, that
of power and authority.

It might be appropriate to begin by noting some dissent on
the nature of collegiate leadership authority. In a paper now almost
a quarter-century old, Terry Lunsford writes "University specialists
in administration today cannot convincingly claim, as a group, any
distinctive experience which clothes their bare, formal positions
with "professional" legitimacy. In the highly professional organization that is a university, this alone means that their very authority
is more or less precarious" (1968, p. 6).

In a later publication (1974), Cohen and March explore the
ambiguity of the college presidency. They conclude that the presidency was a reactive job:

> The presidency is an illusion. Important aspects of the
> role seem to disappear on close examination. In par-
> ticular, decision making in the university seems to
> result extensively from a process that decouples prob-
> lems and choices and makes the president's role more

commonly sporadic and symbolic than significant. Compared to the heroic expectations he and others might have, the president has modest control over the events of college life. The contributions he makes can easily be swamped by outside events or the diffuse qualities of university decision making (p. 2).

Another somewhat cynical view on the exercise of authority in collegiate settings, though one not entirely inaccurate, can be found in Huber's book *How Professors Play the Cat Guarding the Cream.* Huber quotes former University of Hartford president Stephen Trachtenberg (now president of George Washington University) concerning the nature of the exhaustive interviews associated with presidential search and appointment. According to Trachtenberg, his opinions were invited on a range of issues related to teaching, research, learning, and scholarship during the search. Following appointment, however, any presidential expression of interest on these matters was viewed by the faculty with the same favor and welcome as a "tap dancer at a funeral" (Huber, 1992, p. 18). A preoccupation with the process of decision making and the complex web of authority interactions lead Huber to this statement: "Authority in the academy is exercised by a hierarchy of unequal equals that is designed to express opinions rather than to execute the decisiveness of command" (1992, p. 25).

Faculty and staff members, students, alumni, civic and community leaders, political and business leaders, board members—the expectations of so many constituents do indeed constitute a complication for collegiate leadership that might not be associated with some corporate leadership positions. Moreover, colleges and universities are not a "command" enterprise. Of course, there are important limits on the power and the authority of a college president—as anyone who has ever held the position will attest. Colleges and universities are also reverse discretion organizations similar to police forces and hospitals, where decision responsibility rests heavily with the firing-line professional: the officer on the beat, the physician in the operating room, and the professor in the classroom, laboratory, or studio.

Are presidents and other collegiate leaders without authority, afloat on a sea of ambiguity without rudder or sail? What might we say about the posture and the promise of new presidents or other academic administrators entering their positions with the theory that they have taken on jobs both impossible and without authority. What kind of performance reality would such a vision of role produce? From my perspective, college presidents and other university administrators have access to precisely the same forms of authority as leaders in other settings. These include

- Authority of position—the ability to influence behavior by virtue of appointment
- Authority of competence—the ability to influence behavior by virtue of expertise
- Authority of character—the ability to influence behavior by virtue of integrity
- Authority of personality—the ability to influence behavior by virtue of constructive style
- Authority of ideology—the ability to influence behavior by virtue of shared values

Leaders who have no awareness of these multiple sources of authority or who believe that their authority is limited are not likely to become an artist in its use. There are times and places for the exercise of legitimate authority—that of position. There are times and places for the exercise of the softer forms of authority. And there are times for what I call "guerrilla goodness" in the application of authority: the use of leverage.

"Guerrilla goodness" describes the occasional use of unorthodox techniques to achieve desirable goals. As a modest example, consider the following. When a well-respected professor of some thirty years' service moved into his office in a newly constructed office and classroom building, he found that all the office doors were of clear glass, offering little in the way of privacy. His stream of requests for a solid door produced no corrective action. He therefore obtained a print of a painting that portrayed a well-endowed nude woman—a painting that is displayed in an international art museum. He displayed the print on his office door, securing the desired privacy and enhancing the cultural tone of the office suite.

Receiving complaints from many other faculty occupants, but finding no policy against such a display, university officials found it expedient to replace the glass door with a solid one.

The commanding and classic text for those interested in the concepts and application of guerrilla goodness in a variety of settings is Saul Alinsky's 1971 book *Rules for Radicals*. Here can be found wonderfully entertaining stories about how to leverage authority, about how the "have nots" can get the attention of the "have a lots." (One suspects, however, that it would not be as entertaining to be found on the receiving end of Alinsky's tactics.) Let us turn to one of those stories.

Unable to secure the attention of civic leaders in the city of Rochester, New York, concerning the deplorable conditions in a poor neighborhood, citizens invited Alinsky to assist them. In a display of civic and cultural ardor, Alinsky and friends purchased a block of 100 tickets for the next symphony concert in Rochester. A large dinner was held for those 100 ticket-holders prior to the concert—a dinner that consisted in its entirety of generous portions of baked beans. Apparently there was no city ordinance against passing gas in a symphony concert; and, as the newspaper reported the morning after, "It was all over before the first movement. . . ."

Here are two additional collegiate illustrations of guerrilla goodness.

A new college dean was alerted to the possibility that a faculty member had engaged in unwanted sexual advances to female students and colleagues at another institution. One year later, the dean was visited by the administrator of a large area hospital who claimed that this same professor had taken the administrator's freshman daughter to his home, where she was temporarily staying. This might have been less troubling if the professor had been married, but he was not. Apparently, the daughter had become angry over relationships with her stepmother and had left home. The professor had become the informal therapist of the young woman, who was a student in one of his classes. The living arrangement, however, suggested more than a therapeutic relationship. The angry hospital administrator demanded that the dean and university take immediate corrective action.

Attempts to resolve this parental complaint via persuasive

approaches through the department chair elicited a thumbing-of-the-nose response from the professor, who suggested that neither the dean nor any other administrator had any right to meddle with his private behavior. So much for the soft forms of authority. The probable outcome of any directive to the faculty member reminded the dean of a piece of advice he had received as a young second lieutenant: give no orders that will not be obeyed. The dean therefore entertained other options.

In previous years, the faculty had established a grievance procedure intended to serve as an appeal process for professors who felt wronged in matters related to their personal welfare. The dean decided that this faculty appeals procedure might possibly be turned to other purposes. He suggested an informal meeting with the chair and faculty member to advise that if the female student were not removed from his home immediately, he, the dean, would refer the parent's complaint to the faculty grievance committee, where the interests of the parent, the daughter, and the faculty member might receive due consideration. The effect of this move would be to give the poor judgment of the professor public visibility, placing his behavior and judgment in full view of sober-minded and senior members of the university faculty. (The salutary test of public forum will be explored in another chapter on the ideal of candor.)

This referral action never had to be taken, however. Faced with the possibility of a public forum on his behavior and with a predictably unhappy outcome, the professor decided that having the young student leave his home was the better part of discretion. He was reprimanded in writing for exercising poor judgment and for failing to consult with colleagues and others on the campus; for example, the counseling center might have rendered more legitimate and appropriate help to the young student. He was also advised to be grateful that the angry parent was a hospital administrator, who valued health, rather than a Green Beret from the nearby army base, who might have considered a broken arm or leg as an appropriate remedy for wrongful action. Curiosity opens to academic leaders knowledge of the forms of authority and skill in techniques of application. Here a more oblique tactic was better than frontal assault; leverage was more powerful than a battering ram.

Faced with the prospect of no raise for the second year in a row, the faculty senate of a community college met in somber session to consider the merit of another reward option. Since the state was not going to provide the faculty a raise, one proposition advanced was that the faculty arrange a "psychic" raise in the form of a reduction in office hour expectations. Such a proposition was circulated to the faculty, with the suggestion that it entertain this policy proposal at the next meeting of the senate.

The president of the college was placed in a difficult posture. She knew that the area served by the college was experiencing recessionary economic times. A large area industry had recently laid off six thousand workers, and many other people in the region were struggling to hold on to their cars and homes and to put food on the table. She could see that men and women out of work or facing that possibility would hardly be impressed to find that faculty intended to work less for students who would be paying the same or higher tuition—students often dependent upon their parents for help in paying tuition.

Here was a president, however, whose curiosity had taught her that she was not without authority. She considered a range of authority alternatives. One option involved no action on her part at all and was based on the hope that the faculty would sense the folly of the proposal, given what was happening in the community. Resisting the impulse to charge into a policy fray, by the way, is an option of great charm and power for college administrators and one to be more frequently admired and practiced.

A second option was to encourage the faculty in this probability by finding informal moments to exercise the authority of personality with individual professors and with appropriate academic administrators.

A third approach involved a bit of "guerilla goodness," my phrase for the application of leverage. The president could arrange to have the metropolitan press alerted to the time and topic of the faculty senate meeting so that the debate on this issue would take place in the sunshine, with appropriate media coverage (again, the power of public forum).

A fourth option was to exercise the authority of character by asking for permission to speak at the senate meeting to accent the serious civic and financial liability of the proposed policy. And a fifth option was to exercise the authority of position by advising the faculty senate that its vote on this policy would have to be carried to the system's governing board, since the board carried the final authority on matters of policy related to faculty welfare matters in the community college system. The collective wisdom of the faculty prevailed on this issue, and the proposed reduction on work hours was never presented for a vote.

Patience is among the more difficult of personal virtues to acquire but among the more powerful when properly exercised. Here was a president who first trusted the power of shared values among faculty members. As a leadership artist, however, she kept in reserve a range of other authority alternatives in case her assumption proved to be in error.

There are a number of ideas that can enrich the application of these forms of authority. Begin with the softest form of authority is not a bad guide. Inviting colleagues to look at shared responsibility is always appropriate. Looking for exchange options and leverage is another possibility. Respecting the temptation of power and authority is another, and here I want to engage in a conceptual diversion both scientific and philosophic to illustrate again how curiosity creates knowledge and how knowledge strengthens the art form.

Academic leaders who have some familiarity with the experiments in obedience to authority conducted by psychologist Stanley Milgram at Yale University (1965) will enter their positions more sensitive to the thoughtful use of authority and more attuned to the need for disobedience to it as well. The leader who has read Shakespeare's *Measure for Measure* will also tend his or her positional authority with greater care:

> But man, proud man
> Dressed in a little authority
>   Most ignorant of what he's most assured
> His glassy essence, like an angry ape,
>   Plays such fantastic tricks before high heaven
> As make the angels weep [act 2, scene 2, lines 121–126].

The collegiate leader who knows scene 11 from Bertolt Brecht's play *Galileo* (1966) remembers the change in the Pope's authority demeanor as he dons the papal garments, and will be alert against the seduction of power and the abuse of position.

We have lightly touched the conceptual bases of leadership authority. The enlightening and inspiring pages of science and literature await the leader whose curiosity will lead him or her to strengthen the art form of leadership. Other good ideas await the curious leader to help with the tasks of decision making, organization, change and conflict management, and motivation.

Renewing Through Learning

Leaders and their organizations need moments to recharge. Their ideas can fossilize, their values can decay, and their energy can dissipate. Leaders and organizations operating at the top of the curve, at the peak of excellence, can even then begin to experience the rigidity, the entropy that can set upon the healthiest. Serving the demands of the routine can make them its slaves. Giving birth to a new procedure or a policy can blind them to the necessity for change. Living too close to friends and colleagues can shield their promise from perception. The antidote to both personal and organizational fozzilization is renewal, the recharging of personal and collective batteries. Leaders need renewing moments to replenish their reservoir of energy, to reexamine values and convictions, to rethink the merit of objectives, to break the confines of tradition, and to reevaluate policies and procedures.

The conflicting expectations of multiple constituents, the dilemma of ethical issues clothed in shades of gray, the energy demands associated with an endless line of civic and celebrative functions, the drain of ideological and political combat, the loss of solitude, the frustration of cost containment, the hurt of defeat, the pain of ingratitude, the barbs of criticism—how can we count all the factors that can contribute to leadership stress?

Perhaps presidents, and administrators at other levels as well, ought to be temporarily relieved of duty every seven years or so, encouraged or even forced to take a leave, and then brought back home. This change of place and pace, this shift of agenda and attention, should prove renewing.

Campus leaders indulge a range of renewing ventures: making toy soldiers, collecting rocks and coins, playing the organ and piano, building fine cabinets, studying martial arts, climbing mountains, hunting ducks and deer, collecting antique books and toys.

In addition to these outlets and to research interests, there are a host of professional development opportunities available to administrators. Some of these can be found at professional meetings. Madeleine Green and Sharon McDade performed a useful service in bringing these opportunities into more visible and collated form in *Investing in Higher Education: A Handbook of Leadership Development* (1991).

Each leader selects a different renewal menu. I am not sure that I was always effective in revitalizing my mental and physical resources while I was chancellor, but I did try several approaches. In 1978, my wife and I went to Hilton Head Island on our honeymoon. We have been back each year since to enjoy emotional moments and repeated practices in now-familiar places—a dinner alone, early moments on the beach with one another and with our children. I get the Low Country tug in spring of every year and retain fond memories of those special moments in the life of our family. This was a time when I could read those wonderful books that I was too busy to enjoy during the year—novels and poetry and biography and science, books that refurnish the mind and enrich perspective.

I should not omit the pleasure that comes from reading those things that make you laugh, for laughter is a potent engine of renewal. I spent wonderful moments tossing laughter at the Atlantic Ocean as I read these lines from senior English themes in Richard Lederer's *Anguished English* (1987):

- The Egyptians built the pyramids in the shape of a huge triangular cube [p. 10].
- Pharaoh forced the Hebrew slaves to make bread without straw. Moses led them to the Red Sea, where they made unleaved bread, which is bread made without any ingredients. Afterwards, Moses went up on Mount Cyanide to get the ten com-

mandments. He died before he ever reached Can-
ada [p. 11].

- Sir Francis Drake circumcised the world with a 100
  foot clipper [p. 15].
- Bach was the most famous composer in the world,
  and so was Handel. Handel was half German, half
  Italian, and half English. He was very large [p. 20].
- The First World War, caused by the assignation of
  the Arch-Duck by an anahist, ushered in a new
  error in the anals of human history [p. 21].

In addition to family vacations, I also tried to keep some
inquiry, some small-scale research, under way. Two of these inquiries furnished the foundations for books (both written while I served
as chancellor): *The Enemies of Leadership* (1985) and *A Journey of
the Heart* (1991). I found that indulging these writing interests was
stimulating for me.

Travel is a potent and rewarding means of renewal and learning. A professional journey to the former Soviet Union in 1988 was
a significant such moment in my life. Our purpose was to arrange
faculty and student exchanges between American and USSR colleges and universities. On this exchange trip to the Soviet Union,
I joined four other American college presidents in seeing the Soviet
Union on the leading edge of *perestroika* and *glasnost*. Not in our
wildest imagination, however, would we have predicted from our
experience what has transpired over recent years, though there were
clues.

From Moscow to Leningrad (now once again St. Petersburg),
from Riga to Vilnius, from Minsk back to Moscow, we encountered
higher education in four different republics, their cultural life, and
the interests and concerns of educators and students there. For me,
the emotional high point of the trip occurred on a Wednesday evening in the Latvian city of Riga. In Riga, we were taken to a former
church where a forty-voice choral group from the music conserva-
tory presented a concert in two parts. The first half of the program
was a heroic piece celebrating the end of World War II. The second
half offered four pieces rendered in English, including the spiritual
"Go Down, Moses" and a Norman Luboff choral special.

At the end of the regular program, the conductor turned to the audience and spoke in Latvian. Our interpreter alerted me and my four presidential colleagues sitting in the front rows of the hall that the chorus wanted to recognize our presence by dedicating an encore number in our honor. The chorus then launched into a moving rendition in English of "America." Halfway through the piece, unprompted by the conductor, the entire audience joined in song, again in English. So there we were, several thousand miles from freedom's home, listening as a forty-voice chorus and an audience of four hundred sang to us "America, America, God shed his grace on thee." Large tears emerged unbidden and rolled down my face. And as I looked over at E. K. Fretwell, the six-foot-six chancellor of the University of North Carolina at Charlotte, I could see the tears on his face as well. This was a moment to be deeply imprinted in heart and mind, where the meaning and the moment remain to this day. Oh yes, the people of Latvia were accommodated to the Soviet system, but the fires of freedom still burned in their hearts. And on that evening, we were witness to the glow. A renewing moment in the life of five college presidents.

This travel venture, as well as a visiting lecturer opportunity in the People's Republic of China in 1993, kindled new cultural curiosity in my life and enhanced appreciation for the blessings we enjoy in this country. Renewing moments such as these certainly enhanced my intellectual and emotional growth and I think strengthened my capacity for leadership. They make us yearn to provide similar experiences for colleagues and students.

Exploring the Exhilaration of Error

The exhilaration of error—this may seem a strange aspect of the constructive outcomes that result when a learning leader exercises his or her curiosity. The theme I hope to make plain in a moment. One of the primary avenues of learning for leaders in any setting is experience. In earlier remarks, I emphasized leadership as an art form—a conceptual, a performing, and a moral art form. An art form is not perfected in the passive mode; it requires action and practice. Fundamentals take precedence over the flourishes. What begins as a discrete acquisition of knowledge, skill, and value culminates in an integrated and powerful demonstration of mastery. This unconscious and exhilarating merging of mind, heart, and body is at the heart of Csikszentmihalyi's book *Flow: The Psychology of Optimal Experience* (1990).

Yet in the performance of the accomplished artist resides other pleasures and possibilities, hidden in the mistakes of performance. Mistakes remind us of our humanity. And as we have emphasized earlier in these reflections, mistakes are often the source of new thinking and new direction. They are a form of forced imagination and creativity.

I was pleased to see a paper in an issue of the *Journal of Higher Education* entitled "Making Mistakes: Error and Learning in the College Presidency" (Neumann, 1990). Several important ideas emerged from the research reported in this article. One is that the primary source of presidential error was found in the human and relational domain, in dealing with people, as contrasted to more inanimate policy, structural, or task domain. A second finding is that new presidents are understandably more aggressive in getting to know their roles, their people, their institutions—with the discovery inclination becoming more dampened in later years. In a passing note, the research reported in this paper was built on in-depth interviews with thirty-two presidents. While twenty-six of the thirty-two admitted to errors and mistakes, five could recall none. I worry about those five. I wonder whether they have any fun.

Indeed, one might wonder about those who make no mistakes. We have all heard and repeated that to err is human. But are we really comfortable with this reality? Physician-author Lewis Thomas says there is much to commend the promise of our errors and mistakes: "Mistakes are at the very base of human thought, embedded there, feeding the structure like root nodules. If we were not provided with the knack of being wrong, we could never get anything useful done. . . . The capacity to leap lightly across mountains of information to land lightly on the wrong side represents the highest of human endowments. . . . We are at our finest, dancing with our minds, when there are more choices than two" (1979, pp. 37–39). Harking back to our earlier discussion, mistakes and errors are often the source of new directions. If we are alert, we may experience the exhilaration of our errors. And our mistakes may keep us from arrogance.

Not all error and mistakes may be accompanied by exhilaration, however. One of the mistakes I made as chancellor was the assumption I used to guide my initial entry into the community. My theory was that if I participated in activities revealing a civic concern, the community would care for the university financially. I thus welcomed the opportunity to serve on the Chamber of Commerce board of directors, the American Red Cross board, the symphony board, the opera board, the Boy Scouts council, the Better Business Bureau, and a host of ad hoc task forces and committees. This was not a lost investment, as I think it did assist in building partnership bridges between community and university.

But fund raising is both organizational and personal. I delayed in finding and cultivating those personal contacts that might have yielded a stronger dividend in private gifts to the university. We did raise private money, but we might have done much better had I turned to the more personal approach much sooner. Perhaps, as suggested previously, my search and discovery behavior diminished the longer I was in office. This may be one of the reasons why Donald Walker proposes in *The Effective Administrator* (1979) that ten years is a reasonable tenure in the presidency.

There is another form of error that may be associated with experiential learning. It is that our experience may yield superstitious learning. Donald Walker describes the phenomenon of superstitious learning as follows: "A regularity in the operation comes to our attention, an administrative maneuver is "successful" and, bingo, we have a principle. We sound like imbecile owls" (1979, p. 114).

Most institutions have formal commitments to affirmative action in their personnel search and selection processes. A newly appointed president of a public liberal arts college carried to that appointment a keen belief in the validity of affirmative action and was determined to demonstrate that conviction in all searches for which he was directly responsible (those positions reporting directly to the president). In filling six positions over two years, he brought to the college three new faces and talents from outside, and he gave three promising internal talents an opportunity for growth and renewal. The reception accorded this commitment to affirmative action nicely confirmed his judgment that this was a proper way to do business.

Soon, however, the president found himself in a position where a violation of his conviction seemed necessary. In a search designed to find a replacement for the vice president for academic affairs, a cabal of mischievous deans was able to stack the search committee so that it became possible for it to present the president with a limited panel of candidates, which included one or more of these deans. Believing that perhaps there was some merit in the line from Emerson's essay "Self-Reliance" (1929) to the effect that "a foolish consistency is the hobgoblin of small minds," the president aborted this search and moved to appoint a highly respected associate vice president from another campus in the system.

The appointment brought to the campus an experienced and well-accepted candidate, one with new energy and perspective. This unorthodox move on the part of the president also resulted in a number of other salutary outcomes. It produced a couple of surprised and well-behaved deans. It revealed to the faculty and other staff members on the campus a president who complemented thoughtfulness with daring. It also ended any speculation as to whether the president was easily intimidated. Finally, the decision and action revealed a president who manifested a rich vision of the nature of academic authority.

Making Meaning

Leaders have sometimes been perceived as those who help make meaning for others. I rather like that description. Earlier in this chapter, I elected to take an excursion into the realm of authority. Here I propose a brief pause on the topic of motivation, another responsibility of leadership. A leader who knows only about carrots and sticks is not likely to exhibit a very rich display of artistry.

A variety of things may motivate us: fear (Machiavelli, 1955), achievement (McClelland, 1975), decision dissonance (Festinger, 1957), job content (Herzberg, 1966), reinforcement (Skinner, 1953), fear of death (Becker, 1973). Maslow says that there is a hierarchy of motivators, from security to self-actualization (1943). Sagan believes that puzzles and problems are motivators (1977). Rosenthal identifies expectation as a motivator (1973). And Sergiovanni says that duty can motivate (1992).

Collegiate faculties and administrators are no strangers to the use of rewards and incentives. Are these effective in changing personal and organizational behavior? The 1993 book *Punished by Rewards,* by Alfie Kohn, entertains the philosophical question of whether it is right to use rewards and the empirical question of whether it is effective to do so. His philosophical conclusion is that rewards are controlling and confining; his empirical conclusion is that rewards do not produce lasting personal change, only compliance. I am not ready to abandon rewards and incentives as a motivational tool, but I am thinking more soberly about this instrument of motivation as a result of having read Kohn's book.

Of all those who have written on motivation and the human spirit, I admire the work of Victor Frankl (1959), who indicates that man's search for meaning is the grandest motivator of all. His work is built on experience with men imprisoned in Nazi concentration camps in World War II. Here he saw men with no life-threatening physiological problems curl up in the fetal position and die. Here he also saw men with every physiological reason to die hang on grimly and triumphantly to life. His conclusion is that a man who has a "why" for living can endure any "how."

To make meaning for others, of course, one must make meaning for self. The instrument of curiosity allows the learning leader to do that. Educated men and women enjoy four pleasures. The first of these is learning, a pleasure activated by our curiosity. The other three are loving, serving, and creating, all to be engaged in chapters that follow.

4

The Case for Candor

In the 1982–1983 campaign for governor in the state of Louisiana, our student leadership at LSU Shreveport had arranged to host separate appearances for gubernatorial candidates on the campus. When Democratic candidate Edwin Edwards appeared on campus, he showed his usual charismatic personality and worked his political charm on the assembled crowd of students, faculty members, and civic friends from the city. Even those who considered Edwards a politician who walked on the wild side could be found smiling back at the man at some moment during his remarks.

I stood in the back of the crowd glancing over those present and spotted two or three staff members of the incumbent governor, David Treen. I worked my way over to where they were standing. Speaking to one of them whom I had met earlier as one of the governor's staff representatives in Shreveport, I asked why they were present at Edwards's remarks. "We're the truth squad," the staff member responded. "We're here to keep tabs on all that Edwards says to make sure he tells the truth."

To make sure that political opponents tell the truth seems like a laudable goal. The presence of a "truth squad," I suppose, constitutes some commentary on what the opposition felt about the character of Governor Edwards. But the more I thought about the goal and role of these staff members, the more I considered their work a defensive political investment rather than an offensive one. It suggested that incumbent governor Treen was more interested in keeping the other candidate honest than taking his own case to the people. To what extent the outcome was due to such defensive political behavior is a matter of conjecture, but Governor Treen lost this election to Edwards. Perhaps the presence of a truth squad could be seen as an unpleasant commentary on both political candidates.

For purposes of this discussion, the ideal of candor embraces more than being honest and forthright; it means telling the truth. Telling the truth—this seems like such an obvious moral foundation for leadership in any sector of our national life that one must wonder at the need for restatement or elaboration of the obvious. Yet the case for candor in leadership is an interesting and complicated one, related to caring, conflict, community, and character.

Perhaps I can illustrate by telling another political short story. Four years after the just-mentioned election, Governor Edwards was running for reelection and appeared on the campus of LSU Shreveport to dedicate a new building. Although this ceremony was not billed as a political event in the campaign, it was clearly a de facto one. As I sat on the podium awaiting the moment to introduce Governor Edwards, I remained outwardly calm. Inside, however, the emotional bees were buzzing, as I entertained the suspicion that a group of our active Republican students might try to take advantage of the moment to get in a word for their candidates. I envisioned any number of guerilla tactics that might flow from the imagination of our students.

As it turned out, the dedication ceremony was spared any raucous and disruptive showing. Shortly after Governor Edwards began his dedicatory remarks, a lone student nevertheless made his way down to the speaker's podium and handed Governor Edwards a large sign with the message Vote for Livingston emblazoned across the poster board in large letters. Livingston was a United States congressman running for the governor's chair on the Republican ticket. With a quickness of wit that was a trademark of the governor's political acumen and without missing so much as a syllable in his remarks, Edwards picked up the sign, turned it to the audience, and said, "Ladies and gentlemen, this fine young man has given me this piece of political advice to share with you. Now if you can't vote for me, I want you to vote for Livingston, because I can beat him!" He then put the sign down and went on with his remarks, and both Democrats and Republicans smiled. In this campaign, however, the governor's wit could not save him, and he went down to defeat. Candor in leadership is not an effect of the moment. Variables of character and trust, of record and reputation combine in this matter of leadership candor.

The seal of Harvard University is marked by the word *Veritas,* and the motto of the University of Tennessee is You Shall Know the Truth and Truth Shall Make You Free. I do not know how many other colleges and universities over the nation have the ideal of truth carried on their seals, in their mission statements, in their mottos, or in other documents that delineate their distinctive character. The neglect or dishonoring of the ideal of candor by leaders of organizations devoted to the pursuit of truth must be considered a behavior of special regret and sadness. Let us explore the ideal of candor further.

Candor and the Test of Public Forum

Why does telling the truth, the ideal of candor, deserve our salute and allegiance? Why do we know that telling the truth is right and lying is wrong? A little "thought exercise" with any group of friends and students in which this question is posed will easily elicit the foundations for major ethical systems of thought.

Some will cite the Bible or other religious documents. This is rule ethics, where the rightness of an action is determined by written laws and standards. Another will say that candor is right and lying is wrong because our society says that lying violates the principle of social contract and public trust. This is social-contract ethics in which the rightness of an action is determined by the customs, the traditions, the norms of society and community. Others will suggest that candor is right and lying is wrong because of the unhappy and destructive consequences to others. This is end-result ethics; the rightness of an action is determined by its consequences. A fourth group might believe that candor is right and lying is wrong because the human conscience tells us so. This is a personal ethics approach.

Would we argue with the idea that candor builds trust and that lying yields mistrust? Would we dispute the notion that candor inspires confidence and that lying creates suspicion? Would we debate the point that the fabric of our social relationships, the binding force of social contract, depends on candor, on truthfulness in human relationships? Would we argue with the principle that we would not like our trust betrayed by a lie? Would we contest the idea that the absence of candor and the presence of falsehood acts to fracture the foundation of human relationships? The case for candor, then, rests on solid ground whatever ethical system we may utilize to buttress our claim.

Obviously, then, a governing ideal for effective leadership is that of candor, of honesty and forthrightness in presenting the truth. Leaders can tell the truth, or they can lie. Yet is the matter that simple? It would not take an intelligent person very long to construct a moral dilemma in which a lie might serve a higher moral purpose. Writing in her instructive and stimulating book *Lying*, Sissela Bok enumerates several such situations. Will we lie to liars? Will we lie to enemies? Will we lie to our children (is there really a Santa Claus?)? Will we lie to the sick and dying? Will we lie to protect clients? The moral choice is that we must decide either that lying is absolutely wrong under any and all circumstances or that lying under some circumstances may indeed serve a high moral purpose. This is a discomforting dilemma.

For the leader of good intent and integrity, how are such choices to be made? Bok offers a useful test, that of public forum: "The test of publicity asks which lies, if any, would survive the appeal for justification to reasonable persons. It requires us to seek concrete and open performance of an exercise crucial to ethics: the golden rule, basic to so many religions and moral traditions" (p. 98).

The reader may want to refer to our earlier engagement with the reciprocity test in Chapter Two. The test of public forum, when taken with the reciprocity test, may prove to be two of the more useful and powerful moral guides for the effective leader. How will our behavior or our decision play on the prime-time evening news or before a forum of reasonable peers? To assume that all executive behavior may be reviewed in the white glare of public forum is in my mind a reasonable and healthy assumption. Thus, asking this simple question may stay leaders from behaviors having debilitating and destructive consequences.

Truth with Compassion

Point eight in the W. Edwards Deming management method for guaranteeing quality in any enterprise is to "drive out fear." Deming reveals that the word *secure* comes from Latin roots *se*, meaning without, and *cure*, meaning fear or care. Security thus means being without care or fear (1986, p. 59). Having the intent of candor, the spirit of truth within mind and heart must be complemented with an artistic attention to nurturing a climate of candor. Let us now turn to matters of style as it concerns the ideal of candor.

In a 1990 book entitled *Managing from the Heart*, Gerald Bracey and others accent the role of candor in management. Among the five principles that form the foundation for managing by the heart is this one: "Tell me the truth with compassion" (p. 12). An inclination toward candor is a critical moral prejudice for leaders who want to enhance their effectiveness. What are some of the behavioral tactics that might allow us to place the principle of candor into action with maximum constructive effect, to practice telling the truth with compassion?

The first idea is to speak directly to the person involved. Remember the case study cited in a previous chapter—the vice president for academic affairs who indicated that he planned to give all but one of his deans a raise but who had never discussed his intent with the one unfortunate. This avoidance of direct contact and conversation over a matter of personal behavior and consequence is a violation of the principle of candor. When the topics relate to the prickly business of human behavior and performance, we would rather resort to "murder by memo" than to face a colleague in an eyeball-to-eyeball exchange. Honoring the principle of candor requires that we abandon the cowardly indirect approach. There are other principles that fortunately help ease the way when we must face our colleagues.

The second idea is to listen more and talk less, to inquire more and accuse less. When the president of a community college learned that his director of athletics had apparently made a direct approach to the chairman of the college's board of trustees concerning admissions policies for athletes, the president's temper made a quick launch through the roof of his office and the administration building. Happily, there were no bystanders beyond his secretary, and so no one was injured in the explosion. The secretary remained stoically quiet; she had long ago learned the therapeutic value of her role. And to be fair to the president, he had also learned the value of resolving difficult issues in the quieter afterglow of his mercurial disposition.

A few well-directed questions to the director of athletics in a later meeting, and a bit of patient listening, produced an understanding with a win-win solution for both president and the director of athletics. "DWI"—directing while irritated—is generally to be avoided if we want to encourage climates of candor. There is also a Chinese proverb that says that we should not use a hatchet to remove a fly from a friend's forehead. Although hatchets have the commendable properties of being direct and sharp, artistic leaders will have at their command a wide range of other means for cultivating candor.

The third step is not to make enemies of those with whom we disagree. There is a primeval tendency among some leaders to separate people into two camps: those for the leaders and the others: the enemies. To categorize as enemies those with honest differences of opinion on either purpose and process is unnecessarily to court disaster. First, when we make enemies out of those that disagree, we remove any possibility of having them on our team later. When we demean and distance those who dissent, we can hardly expect to call them into our fellowship on another day and issue. Second, we eliminate any possibility of learning from or benefiting from their dissent. And third, we do not change anything.

The fourth step is to be clear in our expectations. This aspect of candor, by the way, marries nicely with the previously enunciated principles of dignity and reciprocity. There is first the responsibility to orchestrate consent on an agenda of common caring. What goals do we plan to work on? Is there a consensus between my colleagues and me on what goals will command our energy and attention? It will hardly prove helpful, or moral, to evaluate the performance of our colleagues on a hidden agenda. If the dean expects the chair to focus on evaluating and revising the department's graduate program while the chair is expending major energy elsewhere, candor has not been achieved, and conflict is predictable.

Establishing clear expectations for goals and their priorities is a fundamental work of candor; open and thoughtful communication concerning the expectations of performance is another. Thoughtful reinforcement for work well done is an expression of candor; careful exploration of work not well done is equally so. A vice president for research disappointed in the behavior and performance of one of her project directors did not serve the principle of candor well by ignoring the lackluster performance of the director or by leaving the director in the dark about her concerns. Discovering but ignoring the fact that the director had been fighting a losing battle with the ravages of alcohol, because this is a difficult problem to engage, served neither the ideal of candor nor that of compassion (to which we will turn in another chapter). These ideals of effective leadership interact with and reinforce one another. Candor will not be found far from the company of dignity and compassion.

A fifth guideline is to develop a variety of styles in conveying the truth, especially those that accent personal responsibility. As we have already seen, interrogatories are often more effective than imperatives. Of our colleagues, we can ask key questions. What is your vision of the goals you would like to work on this year? What is your assessment of your success in achieving these goals? What is your evaluation of why we failed to get the telephone registration system up and running in time for the fall? What is your perspective on why our nursing program has the lowest pass rate of any in the state, and is the pass rate a quality-performance indicator that should occupy our primary attention? Questions are puzzles to be engaged and are therefore more likely to command the constructive energy of our colleagues. Accusations are judgments to be endured and are more likely to produce resistance and enmity.

Years ago, I employed a young man as a research associate. He seemed a promising talent, someone who I thought might build an effective career in collegiate leadership. In an effort to promote that promise, I encouraged him to enroll in graduate work, and he dutifully did. After a year, however, it became apparent that the "production" from his efforts was quite modest. A couple of policy research efforts seemed permanently stalled. We have all heard, before the firing, the comment that Coach John Doe was a nice man but not a coach. Well, this colleague was a nice man but not a policy researcher. I tried to honor all of the ideas I have been exploring on telling the truth with compassion. What he and I discovered together was that his talent was seriously mismatched to task. In a quiet and reflective moment of self-evaluation over a cup of coffee, the colleague confessed that he was not having any fun in his work and that what he really would like to do was to go to law school. Thoughtfully and compassionately orchestrated, candor encourages moments of self-discovery in ourselves and others.

Finally, telling the truth with compassion recognizes that we may encounter moments when withholding the truth is an appropriate behavior. There is a fine line, however, between behavior that is protective and behavior that will deprive our colleagues of an opportunity to grow and take responsibility for their lives. In *The Road Less Traveled,* Scott Peck suggests, "The selective withholding of one's own opinions must also be practiced from time to time in the world of business or politics if one is to be welcomed into the councils of power. . . . The road that a great executive must travel between the preservation and the loss of his or her identity and integrity is extraordinarily narrow, and very, very few make the trip successfully" (1978, p. 62).

Truth and Trust

Over twenty years ago, I published in *Phi Delta Kappan,* a piece entitled "One Foot in the Stirrup" (Bogue, 1972). In this paper, I propose that open communication, the practice of candor, is essential for creating a climate of trust in an organization. A second function of open communication is to govern the balance of power in our organizations. I then cited a comment offered by John Gardner in his 1968 book *No Easy Victories:*

> I would lay it down as a basic principle of organization that the individuals who hold the reins of power

in any enterprise cannot trust themselves to be adequately self-critical. For those in power the danger of self-deception is very great, the danger of failing to see the problems or refusing to see them is ever present. And the only protection is to create an atmosphere in which anyone can speak up. The most enlightened top executives are well aware of this. But I don't need to tell those readers who are below the loftiest level of management that even with enlightened executives a certain amount of prudence is useful. The Turks have a proverb that says, "the man who tells the truth should have one foot in the stirrup" [pp. 42–43].

I had an opportunity to explore the full meaning of this Turkish proverb late in my career as chancellor of LSU Shreveport. In December of 1988, after I had been eight years in office there, the LSU board and president asked me to leave LSU Shreveport and serve as the interim chancellor of LSU Baton Rouge. This invitation came on the heels of a controversy that had racked the LSU Baton Rouge campus following the resignation of the university's previous chancellor. The issue and circumstances are not important to this discussion except that members of the faculty, staff, and board had become split over the issue and the resignation of the chancellor. Since I was within the LSU system but outside the Baton Rouge campus, my interim appointment was seen as a way to smooth the troubled waters while the search for a permanent replacement took place.

On January 1, 1989, I left in Shreveport my wife and three children and my responsibilities as chancellor there and drove to the state capital and the campus at Baton Rouge. I left behind a mostly undergraduate campus with eight buildings, no intercollegiate athletic program, an enrollment of about 4,200, and a budget of $14 million; I began to explore a campus with over one hundred buildings, an enrollment of 26,000, a budget of $250 million, significant advanced graduate and professional programs, and a "big time" intercollegiate athletic program with a budget of $16 million.

The chancellor's office at LSU Baton Rouge was a very large room with a formidable executive desk located in the middle of the room and a large maroon leather "throne" chair situated behind the desk. In one corner of the office were several yellow leather chairs with cracked finish, circa 1920s, and a couple of unappealing and dusty artificial plants. Behind the desk hung a large and command-ing portrait of Huey P. Long, Louisiana's famed populist governor, who looked down on the office scene with patriarchal gaze. And in the bookshelves along one wall were rows of dusty books left from the incumbency of four previous chancellors.

In the stealth of my first night on the job, I shoved the large desk over on the wall, dispatched the throne chair to the hall and replaced it with one of more comfort and modest demeanor, piled up dusty books in the outer hallway, sent Governor Long's portrait back to the university art archives in exchange for a pastoral oil, and persuaded the vice chancellor for business to replace the cracked yellow chairs and artificial plants with some more attractive furni-ture that I then placed in the middle of the office for a conversa-tional center. I was ready for business.

The business arrived early the next morning. Our director of athletics and the chair of the faculty athletic committee had re-turned from the NCAA convention where Proposition 42, as it was labeled, had been adopted; this was a proposition designed to limit scholarship aid to students with marginal academic records. The proposition elicited widespread dissent. Coach John Thompson at Georgetown walked off the basketball court in protest, and LSU basketball coach Dale Brown, whom I had not yet met, was on national TV lambasting the proposition. Southeastern Conference (SEC) presidents held a phone conference to discuss the proposi-tion. As one whose presidential chair was not yet warm, I listened while the other SEC presidents spoke with then-commissioner Har-vey Schiller. Close to the end of the presidential phone conference, I offered the observation that I thought the coaches had seized the public relations high ground and that perhaps we ought to get on the record. The presidents all agreed to send Commissioner Schiller comments that he might use to construct a statement to be released in the names of the conference presidents.

Meanwhile, I felt that the issue was still largely one sided in its public coverage, so I prepared a short statement offering a con-trasting perspective. I invited athletic director Joe Dean and Coach

Dale Brown over for conversation early the next morning to share with them some of these thoughts before I released any public statement or sent my letter to Commissioner Schiller. This honest approach was courteous and also let me ascertain whether there were points of view I had overlooked. This meeting was held at 8:30 A.M.

At eleven o'clock that same morning, the phone on my desk rang, and I took a call from Governor Buddy Roemer. The governor indicated that he understood I had written a letter on Proposition 42. The governor then pronounced that Proposition 42 was bullshit. I suggested to the governor in a tactful but not bashful tone that he really ought to study both sides of the issue before he jumped to conclusions on it. I reported that SEC presidents were encouraging a public discussion but that real debate was impossible when coaches were the only voice being heard. The governor, a Harvard M.B.A., then asked me why Harvard voted against the proposition. And I asked him why Princeton had voted for it, suggesting again the need for public debate.

The governor asked if we could visit further on the issue, whereupon I responded that he was the governor and I would show up at a time and place of his discretion. He replied that he had a luncheon engagement out of the city but would call me back in the afternoon. To make a long story short, the governor did indeed call me back that night at my Baton Rouge apartment where I lived during the week (returning over most weekends to be with my family in Shreveport). I told the governor that I thought it was a foolish investment of his time and energy to be calling me day and night on an athletic policy issue when he had plenty on his hands working with the legislature in trying to find a way out of the state's economic recession and revenue crisis. I also stated that I thought it a peculiar piece of business when the basketball coach of the state's major university could appear on national TV and say whatever he pleased on this issue, but when the chancellor of the university spoke, the governor called. I then discussed some dimensions of the issue that I thought had not been explored in what I considered a one-sided debate to this point. And finally, I remarked that I had been a happy man in Shreveport and did not ask for the assignment as interim chancellor in Baton Rouge. But once it was accepted, I would express my loyalty to him and others to whom I was responsible by being forthright no matter what the issue was. The story ended on a happy note with the governor remarking that he could not ask for anything more and that I should call him if I needed him. The governor and I exchanged gifts of candor.

Effective leaders know that loyal candor and dissent keep us from the dangers of groupthink and enrich the elegance and imagination of solutions to the policy and program issues placed before us. Unfortunately, research clearly reveals, that while dissenting perspectives are helpful, we remain uncomfortable with the messenger, the dissenter. In group experiments on this theme, Shepard (1964) shows that, on the one hand, groups having dissenting voices produce richer solutions to problems; on the other hand, if asked to reduce their membership, groups choose the dissenter-deviant as the member to leave. Collegiate executives who sit around conference tables with sycophants, a clump of chums chosen for their comfortable fit, will remember that the cause of candor may not be served by such an assembly. They will value as well those colleagues who appear to have "one foot in the stirrup."

A final note: candor and courtesy constitute useful guides for relating to the press and other media professionals. After one unfavorable headline or encounter, it is easy for some collegiate leaders to consider the press their enemy. This is a mistake in philosophy and value disposition. An opportunity to develop a trusting relationship with the press, one that may be needed later, is lost. Moreover, a competent reporter will find another way to obtain the information that you are trying to withhold. One can find as many unthoughtful and mean-spirited individuals in journalism as in other professions, including academia. However, our schools and colleges and a free press are the essential elements of a democracy. Partnerships built on candor rather than mistrust are helpful to both sectors and to our society.

A Culture of Candor

One of the more recent developments in the evolution of leadership thought and research has been the study of culture. Some scholars such as Schein (1985) suggest that one of the primary role responsibilities of leaders is the management of culture. In *Reframing Organizations,* Bolman and Deal (1991) offer as one of their four frames the symbolic frame, the organization as theater. The unspoken but widely held assumptions and values of a unit or organization constitute its culture. There are myths, rituals, symbols, and stories of the heros of the culture. Frequently cited stories of Dr. Andy Holt, former president of the University of Tennessee, continue to convey several cultural themes—of personal concern for each and every student, of gentle but high expectations for each and every member of the staff, of the university as servant of the state of Tennessee and its people.

An emerging dimension of culture for collegiate organizations, at least those in the public sector, is clearly the widespread availability of information. In *The Knowledge Executive* (1985), Harlan Cleveland, a former college president and dean, suggests that hierarchies of power based on control, those of influence created by secrecy, those of class arising from ownership, and those of politics based on geography are crumbling today.

In public institutions, salary profiles that used to remain hidden in the president's or dean's desk drawer are now found in the library and often find their way into media stories. The sharing of information involves the sharing of power, and this is part of the new culture of collegiate leadership. There is a correlate of that new culture, however: the sharing of responsibility (an idea to which I will return in a moment).

At LSU Shreveport, we kept a copy of the operating budget in the library, and we also placed there end-of-year expense reports and financial balance sheets. Any member of the faculty or staff could see the financial-intent plan of the university and the way the money was spent during the year. In addition, we annually published a fact book on university activities and achievements. This book carried longitudinal-trend profiles on enrollments, personnel, finances, facilities, and student aptitude and achievement profiles (ACT scores and so forth). Finally, we published each year the previous year's salaries, any raises awarded and their reason (equity or merit adjustment, promotion or degree completion), and the current salary for every member of the faculty and staff.

When I arrived at the university, deans and chairs had no

information on the relative enrollment patterns and instructional productivity of their department or college vis-à-vis other units. I had the Office of Institutional Research prepare a complete profile for each department that included credit-hour production profiles by instructional level and faculty equivalents—actual and projected based on instructional activity and other assignments. This openness with information created conflict. And it should have. Those departments that had been carrying heavy instructional loads now began to lobby for a more equitable allocation of faculty lines. Full professors were able to see that as a class their salaries were significantly lower than regional and national averages for other ranks, and so the full professors also began to lobby for justifiable attention.

A culture of candor, then, recognizes that information on activity and achievement in a college or university should be—and will be—more broadly shared than in the past. This is another expression of the public forum test earlier mentioned. Collegiate leaders will be more willing to be "up front" with their faculties and with the public concerning matters of resource allocation.

There is a corollary, as I have noted, to this culture of candor. It requires a culture of responsibility. Those who have access to knowledge carry responsibility for stewardship. In the final year of my appointment at LSU Shreveport, we enjoyed a happy financial situation after eight years of significant financial strain. In the 1990–91 fiscal year, the legislature made available sufficient funds for an average 12 percent raise for the faculty and staff. But state guidelines for the allocation of these dollars stipulated that we would make every effort to compensate those faculty members who had been disadvantaged by market conditions. For my campus, this meant attention to the full professors, since they had served the university the longest and had suffered the most during the many years of recession. It also meant more attention to faculty in arts, sciences, and education than in business, where the market had favored the faculty members we had employed. A college or university may find it difficult to avoid the forces of the market, the influence of supply and demand, but it can ameliorate these.

Once we had the money in hand, I assembled the provost, the deans of the university, and the executive leadership of the faculty senate and asked them to construct a protocol for the allocation of raises to each college, a protocol that would honor the need to compensate for the factors of market and years of service. I expressed my confidence that they could do so and reminded them of what a nice problem it was to have 12 percent salary money to work with.

One member of the faculty executive committee was a bright member of our biology department. Because our salary data were public, he had been able to place each faculty member's salary into his personal-computer memory and develop an allocation algorithm, one that attended to the salary differential by rank and field; this was based on distance between individuals' actual salary by rank and discipline and the regional average.

The application of this algorithm enabled the faculty and administrative panel to calculate the dollars needed to make faculty members by college and by rank within college equidistant from the regional average. This package of dollars was then allocated to the college where deans and chairs made individual salary decisions based on merit (performance) and equity issues (gender, market, rank). Thus, several good principles were honored. The allocation algorithm made it possible to recognize and appropriately reward classes of faculty by rank and discipline without an "across the board" scheme that would have failed to recognize differences in individual faculty performance and equity needs. It was a neat piece of work that represented a splendid act of teamwork between faculty leadership and the academic administration.

The allocation policy was formally approved by the faculty senate and by the deans, actions that proved to be important later in the year. As the fall term got under way, I was visited by a delegation of assistant professors who expressed the belief that they had been shortchanged. For the most part, these assistant professors were those who had not earned a doctoral degree but had served the university well and faithfully over a long period of time. They were certainly deserving, but the allocation protocol recognized as a matter of first priority those faculty members who had earned the doctoral degree. Here was a case where the administration could not be accused of being unfair because the faculty had been its partner in developing the policy. Since the policy had been unanimously endorsed by the faculty senate (having as members assistant professors without doctoral degrees), I suggested that this concern be laid before these professors' peers! A culture of candor thus encourages a culture of shared responsibility.

Not all is simple in the new culture where openness, participation, and candor are key, however. Cleveland (1985) comments on the difficulty: "Experience teaches that the procedures of openness are well designed to stop bad things from happening and ill designed to get good things moving, unless the consensus for action has been built in private ahead of time" (p. 53).

In their enlightening and integrating work on personal and organizational change, *Breakpoint and Beyond* (1992), George Land and Beth Jarman suggest that there is a creative dynamic as individuals, organizations, and societies move through three stages of evolution. There is first the forming stage, marked by an entrepreneurial, divergent, and creative spirit. Phase two, the organizational norming state, characterized by the search for order; this stage includes the development of management and policy systems. As an example, Henry Ford brought the automobile industry into the second phase by standardizing manufacturing. Here in the second phase, we find the traditional command-and-control inclinations of leadership and management thought.

In phase one we have the entrepreneur—the "maniac with a mission," as Land and Jarman say it—while after the "breakpoint" leading to the second phase we find the professional manager with his or her bag of management tools (management by objectives, program budgeting, and total quality management). Instead of a "maniac with a mission," we have what I describe as a "manager with a measure" (if I might take the liberty of interpreting some of Land and Jarman's commentary). The authors furnish an example from collegiate life: "Even in the halls of academe the measurements have also become the mission. The 'publish or perish' syndrome forces faculty members seeking tenure to put most of their emphasis on research and writing rather than teaching, even though the claim is continually made by university officials that teaching is a professor's most important contribution" (1992, p. 47).

When I came to the University of Tennessee in the fall of 1991, one of the first steps in "getting on board" was to have one's car registered in the university police office and to secure the all-important parking "hunting" permit. As I handed my completed application form to the woman behind the window in the campus police office, she said to me, "Dr. Ernest Grady Bogue! And what will you be doing for the University of Tennessee, Dr. Ernest Grady Bogue?"

"Well," I began, "I will be teaching . . . " But before I could complete my sentence, she interrupted.

"Dr. Ernest Grady Bogue, do you mean that you don't intend to do any research for the University of Tennessee?"

"Yes, I do hope to be involved in research," I replied, "but I also intend that teaching will have the first call on my time and talent."

"Dr. Ernest Grady Bogue," the police woman repeated in heavy and marked tone, "do you realize, sir, that you are the first person who has purchased one of my fine parking decals this morning who was willing to admit that he was going to teach anything for the university?"

When this kind of exchange takes place in the campus police office, we can make some inferences about the reward structure and culture of the university. One of the more helpful works on this tension in the research university is Gerald Graff's *Beyond the Culture Wars* (1993). Graff observes that "it is time to recognize that arriving at consensus is not the only way to pull a curriculum together, that difference can be a basis for coherence (and community) if it is openly engaged rather than kept out of sight" (p. 58). Thus, his book is not only a useful commentary on teaching-research tensions and political correctness debates, but it also affirms the ideal of candor.

Returning to Land and Jarman's book, the authors point out that many organizations surviving phases one and two will not manage the new breakpoint change to stage three. Though a transportation industry, for example, railroads did not invent airplanes. An early entrepreneur in retailing, Sears experienced difficulty in making the transition to new realities. The giants of the American automobile industry were at the top of their success curve when foreign competitors began to make marketing inroads on new principles of quality, customer interests, and production efficiency. There are some pleasant turnaround stories in each of these three industries.

In phase two, most organizations are too preoccupied with improving current products and processes to nurture the imaginative and inventive thought that will produce new products and services. As Land and Jarman remark, "Today, the public schools, large mature businesses, the transportation industry, the energy industry, medicine, and the legal system, to name just a few, need groups totally dedicated to the question, 'how can we reinvent ourselves?'" (p. 58). Emphasizing that "nothing fails like success," Land and Jarman remind us that organizations at the peak of their success in any industry are prime candidates to become organizational dinosaurs. Does this idea have implications for American higher education?

To address that question, let us relate all this commentary to the theme at hand, that of candor. Land and Jarman suggest that the new rules for phase-three organizations, those in the fulfilling stage, will include divergence and integration, shared leadership, and integration of differences. These organizations will replace "conflict and competition with trust and cooperation" (p. 119). A bit further in their book, the authors add that successful organizations in phase three will be those in which secretive or guarded leadership behavior gives way to open, honest, forthright behavior. And still later, they comment that creative organizational climates are described by those living in them as places where "we were open with each other and told the truth" (p. 146).

The evolution of the American university has been a breakpoint one in which the instructional and research emphases of the British and German models have been married to that peculiar pragmatic American spirit. The result has been the creation of the public and professional service mission. And the development of the two-year community college constitutes another breakpoint in higher education. Will the next imaginative and inventive developments in higher education come from within the academy? Not without the spirit of candor. And even when collegiate leaders do cultivate a culture of candor, history teaches us to doubt if conventional wisdom will allow us sufficient detachment and freedom to give birth to the new ideas that will take us to a phase-three organization.

Candor and Credibility

Toward the end of *Breakpoint and Beyond,* Land and Jarman comment that "values have been thought of as the soft stuff of the organization, something that goes on a bronze plaque in the front corridor. Somehow the values get separated from how the business really runs" (1992, p. 187). This is a reminder of what sensitive and effective leaders have always known: what our policy manuals say is far less important than how we live. Boyer emphasizes the same theme when he comments in *College: The Undergraduate Experience* that the principal challenge of our time is that conscience has become separated from competence (1987, p. 111). Our opening comments in Chapter One affirm the reality of this dichotomy in the lives of too many collegiate leaders. Candor is an instrument for reconciling competence and conscience.

In their 1993 book *Credibility,* Kouzes and Posner accent the need for credible leaders, ones who are "honest, forward looking, inspiring, and competent" (p. xx). They propose that credibility is developed through six practices, the disciplines of credibility: discovering self, appreciating constituents, affirming shared values, developing capacity, serving a purpose, and sustaining hope. Candor is an essential ideal in fostering these disciplines of credibility.

Candor entails a disposition toward compassionate conveyance of the truth. Truth is the foundation for trust. And trust is the principal building and bonding force of all organizations, especially for those whose mission is the pursuit of truth.

5

The Touch of Compassion

I would like to edit the dictionary definition of the word *compassion* for purposes of this chapter. By compassion, I mean a sympathetic concern and an active caring. But a concern and a caring for what? The first, the most obvious, and the most appropriate object of the leader's sympathetic concern and active caring would certainly be those colleagues who give life and meaning to the unit or organization entrusted to his or her care. Beyond this expectation, however, the leader's concern and caring should also extend to climate and community, to the context in which colleagues will labor. And finally I would suggest that the leader's concern and caring should embrace standards of performance and excellence, points of principle if you will.

Love 'Em and Lead 'Em

The compassionate leader is a loving leader. Browsing through book indexes is not a routine activity of mine, but I thought that it might prove interesting to see how frequently the term *love* appeared in the indexes of books on leadership. The reason for my curiosity was that it appeared to me that the word was appearing with increased frequency in more recent publications on leadership.

For example, in a work I introduced in Chapter Four, *Breakpoint and Beyond,* authors George Land and Beth Jarman offer the principle of trust and love as one essential to the management of organizations that are to survive breakpoint changes with the past. Yet they are mindful of the risk involved with the insertion of love into the management lexicon: "Oh, how well we know the trepidation of using the 'L word.' Love is hardly the word you would expect to find in the world of organizations. In fact, both authors have been asked by some corporate executives to not use the word love" (Land and Jarman, 1992, p. 205).

In one of the better books on leadership role, one that I use in a number of my seminars on the subject, Kouzes and Posner support the leadership dimension of love in a chapter called "Encouraging the Heart": "We once asked U.S. Army Major General John H. Stanford to tell us how he would go about developing leaders, whether at Santa Clara University, in the military, or in private business. He replied, 'When anyone asks me that question I tell them I have the secret to success in life. The secret to success is stay in love. Staying in love gives you the fire to really ignite other people, to see inside other people, to have a greater desire to get things done than other people'" (1987, p. 270). In the opening of this chapter, Kouzes and Posner quote the general as suggesting this leadership guide: "Love 'em and lead 'em." When a general of the army is connecting two *L* words, *love* and *leadership,* one has to think seriously about the merit and validity of the connection.

Another contemporary writer on leadership, Peter Koestenbaum (1991), offers this insight on the contribution of love to leadership effectiveness: "We all recognize the importance of love in life—how we need it to be happy, to grow, even to be healthy. But, regrettably, many people feel it has no place in business. Love means that you really care about people, whether you are a mother or a general. To love is to communicate intimately in the sense of establishing an intersubjective field, a joint ego or communal self. Love establishes a higher unity, a spiritual connection, an emotional bond" (p. 167). *Love, spiritual, emotional*—are these not interesting words for books on leadership, management, and organization? We should add another: *calling.*

Writing in *Love and Profit* (1991), James Autry suggests that there are two kinds of managers: (1) "those who practice management as a trainable skill" and (2) "those who approach manage-

ment as a calling"(p. 13). The word *calling* we more often associate
with those ministerial professions where God has perhaps whis-
pered in the ear of those entering the profession. Autry goes on to
suggest that a title and an office only make a boss. He describes
management and leadership as a sacred trust.

And here is a surprising context for the word *love*. Writing
in *Leadership and Jazz*, Max Depree says, "One of the many pacts
of love that a leader upholds is to make the organization accountable to the plan" (1992, p. 30). How many times have we seen the
terms *planning* and *loving* connected?

As I browse through the indexes of leadership literature, I
therefore conclude that the ideal of compassion is one relatively new
in its conceptual celebration. One does not find the words *compassion* or *love* with significant frequency in literature prior to the
1980s, and one might even conclude that the terms are more often
to be found in books released in the past five to seven years. At least
one significant exception I will explore in a moment.

Let us restate our theme. Corporate or collegiate, the leadership of any organization involves technical and personal competen-
cies. If the ticket agent or flight attendant of my airline flight is
crusty and cranky, then the aerodynamic sophistication of the air-
craft may not compensate for my sour response. But if an engine on
that plane quits between Knoxville and Dallas, I am interested in
survival, not courtesy; the technician who can keep those jet engines
humming can be a human relations sourpuss of the first degree. If
the director of financial aid is service personified but my aid check
arrives four weeks after registration, her splendid attitude may not
compensate. Thus, the leader must have concern and caring for
both the personal resources of the organization and for its technical
performance standards.

The Problem of Administrative Compassion

As earlier noted, in this discussion I will frequently use the term
compassion and love in connection. By compassion and love, I
simply mean the leader's sympathetic and active caring for people
and principle.

I began thinking seriously about the role of compassion in

leadership many years ago. In *Without Sympathy or Enthusiasm: The Problem of Administrative Compassion* (1975), scholar Victor Thompson proposes that organizations cannot issue compassion but individuals can. Is this so? Who among us has not faced some exasperating experience with organized enterprise, on either the giving or receiving end? Years ago, when I was a young registrar, we had a capable young student, a senior with a 3.5 GPA, who contracted mononucleosis in late summer. His illness simply would not permit him to register for the fall term until classes had been in session for almost a week. Given his academic record, I granted an exception and gave him permission to register past the deadline. A few days later, I received a phone call from a professor who gave me an angry verbal lashing for allowing this student to enter his class late. He was not interested in the student's record or promise. He had not troubled himself to talk to the student. He was only interested in following the rules.

In pleasant contrast, I cite another professor who had in his class a young woman who, in the middle of the fall term, began to have serious family difficulty, which culminated finally in a divorce. Because of family obligations, the student was no longer able to attend class in the evening. Rather than see the student lose her investment in the course, the professor undertook to tutor the student during the day each remaining week of the term. A sympathetic caring.

Actually, in the first illustration, there is another important point, and an argument might be made that I was wrong and the professor right. Victor Thompson poses this question: "Can modern organizations be compassionate? Can they 'care'?" (1975, p. 8). His answer to the question is no. Thompson suggests that "in the final analysis, compassion is an individual gift, not an organizational one" (p. 13). And, according to Thompson, the reason is that "to recognize compassion in administration is to recognize another claim; it is to 'steal' the owner's property" (p. 10). Thompson frowns on the "Robin Hood" vision of leadership in modern organizations, that leaders are to use their special position to take from those who have money and power and give to those who do not.

According to Thompson, all organizations have "owners." We do not always enjoy thinking about that in colleges and universities, this "we-them" mentality. It is worth remembering, however, that boards of trustees do in fact hold the university in trust. The forums of the people, their legislatures, appropriate the funds so that governing boards can exercise this special trust, at least for public institutions, including public colleges.

In a state that had experienced several years of revenue reductions, a continuing recessionary climate offered the prospect of yet-additional cuts, with some legislators suggesting that these might run as high as 30 percent for higher education. In a moment of understandable frustration, the president of a public university in this state closed it down for a day so that students and faculty members might travel to the capital to lobby the legislature. The "owners" were not happy, however, with this act of stewardship and subsequently summoned the president to the capital for a day-long arduous session with the budget committee. The legislators complained that they thought public funds were made available to the university so that school would be held rather than being used to support the lobbying efforts of faculty and students.

Is Thompson right then? If leaders exercise compassion, are they in fact "stealing" from the owners of an organization? Well, I think that Thompson's point is worth remembering. At the same time, I believe that leaders can still exercise compassion without creating what Thompson calls the problem of compassion. In allowing that student to register a couple of days late, I may have violated official policy of the university, but I am not sure that I stole anything of value from any of its owners. And if there are to be no judgments, no exceptions, then we can simply replace all administrators with computers—an option of commendable efficiency that might be welcomed by some faculty members who think administrators are a nuisance anyway and by some legislators who think that we should spend less money on administration. This less personal approach will work well until a faculty member or a legislator begins to look for a moment of exception in the policy or program life of the college or university.

The president of a research university experienced a personal instance of conflict with political constituents on a matter of university policy, a case illustrating the difficulty of representing a sympathetic caring for both person and principle. An assistant professor in one of the university's academic departments had been recommended for promotion to associate professor and tenure on a split call of departmental senior faculty members, who had turned him down the previous year. The department chair and dean of his college recommended against promotion and award of tenure, as did the university provost. The president knew little or nothing about the esoteric specialty of the faculty member in question and sustained the negative recommendation.

The faculty member petitioned for an appeal to the university's board of trustees, which the president promptly forwarded to the board. Here, however, matters began to get more complicated. This professor was engaged to a woman prominent in community social and civic circles. The social network led to features of the case's being communicated to an attorney who was both a member of the board and a member of the academic affairs committee that was to hear the appeals presentation. Meanwhile, the dean and provost learned that the attorney member of the board intended to recommend that the matter be arbitrated by an external third party.

When the president, the provost, and dean appeared before the board committee, five members of the board academic affairs committee occupied their elevated position at the dais reserved for them. The president was in his chair at the desk reserved for system presidents, with the provost and dean sitting behind. On the other side were the assistant professor and his attorney. And in the back of the room, sitting quietly by herself, was the faculty member's fiancée.

As expected, the attorney member of the committee opened the inquiry by indicating that in cases where there appeared to be irreconcilable differences, lawyers were inclined to seek resolution in the form of outside arbitration. He then began shaking his head up and down in the affirmative fashion and asked the president if he would consent to arbitration. The president responded by shaking his head left and right and indicated, as tactfully but assertively as he could, that he would not consent.

The president stated that what the board members had before them was a sharp difference of opinion. The faculty member felt that he was qualified for associate professor and tenure, and those campus faculty and academic administrators the board had entrusted to make academic judgments did not. Then the president continued with the observation that the faculty member had enjoyed access to the same procedures of review and evaluation—and to routes of academic appeal—that had been accorded hundreds of faculty members before him. He summarized by saying that campus officers had exercised their trust and responsibility by making their best judgment on the case and there they would stand. But he also recognized and respected the right and authority of the committee to recommend rejection of the campus's recommendation or to invoke an arbitration procedure. Afterwards, the other four committee members voted against the attorney and sustained the recommendation of the university.

Now there are several ideas of importance here. One is that compassion means more than caring for clients and colleagues; it also means caring for standard and principle, for equity and excellence. And the second is that collegiate administrators need to remember that they live at the "feet" of the people. From my perspective, lay oversight of professional insight is a historic and constructive dimension of governance in American higher education. Though on any given issue or day, board supervision of college leaders' decisions may prove moderately discomforting or downright painful, the relationship is a healthy one. In *Governing Public Colleges and Universities*, Ingram and Associates (1993) note that "the citizen board has emerged as the best alternative to governmental or exclusive faculty control of higher education. As imperfect as they are, governing boards have proven their value in the U.S. version of participatory democracy, which is averse to monopoly of power and which provides systems of checks and balances" (pp. 3-4).

Returning to Victor Thompson's claim that organizations do not exhibit compassion but that individuals can and do, I want to think about that assertion a bit. It seems to me that organizations do seek to show caring for those who give them life. They make place for administrative exceptions to policy. Otherwise, we could, as I have noted, replace all administrators with computers. Moreover, organizations will usually have appeals processes on most matters related to employee welfare, so that personal and extenuating circumstances may be properly considered. Organizations will also frequently establish services such as day care to support their employees. And I know of one corporation that plans to open an elementary school adjacent to one of its large manufacturing plants, a school to serve the children of its employees. Organizations are more frequently attending to personal and family connections in other ways—as, for example, in the use of flextime. Organizations offer a range of employment assistance and referral services and make training and development investments in their employees. It may be argued that any and all of the support services are self-serving investments on the part of the organization. To care for others is to care for self, however.

In her book *When Giants Learn to Dance,* Rosabeth Moss Kanter furnishes an interesting perspective on the historic position of organizations: "Historically and cross-culturally, organizations of all kinds, especially those making a radical break with the past, have attempted to exclude or neutralize particular ties that might compete with the loyalty and the commitment the organization demands from its members. The family is an especially insidious source of competing loyalties" (1989, p. 286). But a few pages later, she suggests that organizations must adopt a new posture:

> As organizations loosen up and begin to operate on less hierarchical premises, giving more people an opportunity to participate in decisions, tackle challenging projects, and take on exciting tasks, they also become more absorbing of people's time, energy, and emotions. If they are allowed to absorb more of the person without providing support for other responsibilities, they will either become more antagonistic to the family than they have been in the past or eliminate the prospect of ever reaching equal opportunity goals in the more challenging, higher-level, and better paying positions [pp. 293–294].

Colleges and universities are not immune to the tension between work and family. A new college president took appointment following a known workaholic, a frenetic former executive who would think nothing of calling his staff at midnight on a routine and regular basis, asking for answers to questions or directing that

some action be taken first thing in the morning. This was a collegiate executive who worked most evenings, most Saturdays, and
parts of Sunday on a regular basis. Whether this occasioned tension
and neglect in his own family life is a matter of speculation, but it
was sure that he created tension and neglect in the family life of his
staff, which he expected to be present when he was at the university.

In his first meeting with staff members, the new president
suggested that they should not bother him at home or after 6:00 P.M.
unless they had something really important to discuss. In turn, he
would not interrupt their family life unless he too had something
very crucial to justify the interruption. He then observed that if they
could not run the college in a decent set of work hours, they were
ill organized, ill staffed, or short on intellect and imagination. If
any of these potential problems actually existed, it was up to him
to solve them. And it was so. An old and weary team became a new
one, caring for and furnishing effective leadership to the university
and to the individual families concerned.

Let us sum up here. A leader's compassion will extend to the
welfare and promise of clients and colleagues, those who revolve
within the circle of her or his special trust. The compassion of leaders will extend also to points of principle and policy as they strive
to reconcile the special needs of their organizations, faculty and staff
colleagues, clients and "owners," and families. Both leaders and
their organizations can attend to the design ideal of compassion.

High Tech and High Touch

Those living in the twentieth century can scarcely deny the dramatic
effects of technology in their lives—airplane and space travel, computers, nuclear power, lasers, microcircuitry, genetic engineering,
antibiotics, and the marriages of these technologies. In his first book
on transforming trends (1982), John Naisbitt suggests that when a
new technology is inserted into our lives there must be a counter-
balancing personal and human concern. High tech begets the need
for high touch.

The caring little touches mark the art form of each leader. An
awareness of family, a friendly call or card on birthdays, will elevate
the spirit of many of our colleagues. A little slower walk into the

office each day to catch up on the latest in family news or the health condition for an ailing colleague is an easy but constructive investment in caring. Peters and Waterman recommend in their book *In Search of Excellence* "management by walking about" (1982, p. 122). This practice gets managers out of their offices into the engine rooms of the organization so that they can gather the informal intelligence that will not come their way through memos and the formal chain of communication. This informal contact is a wonderful way to learn about the organization and its people.

When I was appointed interim chancellor of LSU Baton Rouge in January of 1989, one of the first steps I took to understand this large enterprise was to spend informal moments wandering around the university early, mid, and late. I remember visiting the six-story biology building one afternoon about 4:30 P.M. As I passed one departmental office, I paused and introduced myself to a faculty member there. This professor then led me on a fascinating tour of the building, the program, and the faculty. From the overtaxed storage area in the basement, to the labs on the top floor where rats yielded research information through brain implant sensors, to a floor with refrigerators occupying hallway space, this was a learning journey that I would never have experienced any other way. And I gained a perspective that was at once more direct, personal, and meaningful than any written communication might have conveyed. And I made a friend on the botany faculty. I still have fond memories of Dr. Russ Chapman and the journey we took on that day.

A midmorning visit to the Louisiana Press on a later walking tour gave me an opportunity to learn the story behind *A Confederacy of Dunces* (Toole, 1982). Here was a work of fiction whose author, James Toole, had seen his work rejected by almost every major publisher in the country. Following his unfortunate death by suicide, the LSU Press published the book, whose story unfolds in New Orleans. The book subsequently won the Pulitzer Prize for literature.

The important point of this walking tour, this informal sensing of the organization, was that I gained additional access to the soul of the university. But I also hope that I also reinforced those colleagues whose lives I touched but a moment. And so a simple means of exhibiting concern and caring is to walk a little slower, a little more often, and a bit further.

A friend who is a college vice president tells me of one of these informal walks he took one day. He happened to catch one of his college deans at a moment of high family stress. The dean's wife had experienced serious and life-threatening surgery and remained on the critical-condition list. The dean and his wife were without immediate family in their relatively new university setting; they had moved to the university only one year previously. When the president entered the office of the dean and inquired, "How're you doing?" the dean began to cry. The vice president walked around behind the dean's desk and hugged him for several moments until the crying subsided. A touch of compassion. A passing moment of opportunity that would not have occurred unless the vice president had been out of his office experiencing the university in this informal fashion.

A form of compassion that is not a reaction to technology but one well based in human relations research is high leadership expectations. I introduced this theme in Chapter One, where I suggested that leadership expectations contribute to the construction of social realities. There is philosophy, and there is empiricism. There is the philosophy of Goethe, and there is the research of Rosenthal and Livingston. Goethe suggests that to accept people as they are results in their becoming worse, whereas to accept people for their promise helps them realize that promise. In *Sand and Foam*, Gibran observes that "there is a space between man's imagination and man's attainment that may only be traversed by his longing" (1973, p. 11). Many leaders are now familiar with the research of Rosenthal (1973) in both experimental psychology and in school-based settings, research clearly demonstrating that the quality of our expectations is a key determinant in the kind and quality of behavior we elicit from students. In a business-setting replication, Livingston (1969) also demonstrates the power of expectancy theory.

These philosophical and empirical foundations for the power of leader expectations are complemented by artistic expressions. The Greek myth of Pygmalion provided the theme for George Bernard Shaw's play *Pygmalion*, which (as we saw earlier) furnished the inspiration for the Lerner and Loewe musical *My Fair Lady*. In the middle of Shaw's play are these lines from the Cockney flower girl Eliza: "You see, really and truly, apart from the things anyone can pick up (the dressing and the proper way of speaking, and so on), the difference between a lady and a flower girl is not how she behaves, but how she's treated. I shall always be a flower girl to Professor Higgins, because he always treats me as a flower girl, and always will; but I know I can be a lady to you, because you always treat me as a lady, and always will" (1969, p. 80). This lovely interaction of philosophy, science, and art adds force to the idea that leader expectations are a critical determinant in the behavior we elicit from our colleagues.

The touch of leader expectations, then, is that of compassion. It is a touch of trust and caring that offers the opportunity of transport, to evoke from a colleague a new level of performance and behavior. Expecting the best of our colleagues, however, is not a guarantor of success in every case; it simply enhances the probabilities. Counting on the best from our colleagues is not an instrument to be employed to make them prisoners of our expectations but rather to nurture their potential and promise. Expecting the best is not the same as making achievement sound easy. And expecting the best of our colleagues does not protect us from betrayal and failure. The possibility of betrayal on the part of a few is the price we are willing to pay for elevating the performance and the promise of the many.

Via the power of expectations, the collegiate leader thus extends his or her caring and compassion to each client and colleague who moves within the circle of his or her responsibility. Compassion is nurtured in units of one. But there is another field awaiting the attention of the compassionate leader. In several places in this volume, I have argued that effective leaders realize that good people can be imprisoned by bad systems. Colleges and universities are more than clusters of monastic cells and individual academic entrepreneurs, where faculty members pass one another in infrequent and impersonal contact, where absence is more often noticed than presence. Let us turn to the idea that leaders care for and cultivate community.

An Agenda of Common Caring:
Compassion and Community

Of the many policy reports that have been issued by the Carnegie Foundation for the Advancement of Teaching over recent years, one that I found especially relevant to my life as both a college chancellor and now as a faculty member is the monograph *On Campus Life: In Search of Community* (1990). The Carnegie report suggests that there are six principles that should define the collegiate community:

- First, a college or university is an educationally purposeful community, a place where faculty and student share academic goals and work together to strengthen teaching and learning on the campus.
- Second, a college or university is an open community, a place where freedom of expression is uncompromisingly protected and where civility is powerfully affirmed.
- Third, a college or university is a community, a place where the sacredness of the person is honored and where diversity is aggressively pursued.
- Fourth, a college or university is a disciplined community, a place where individuals accept their obligations to the group and where well-defined governance procedures guide behavior for the common good.
- Fifth, a college or university is a caring community, a place where the well being of each member is sensitively supported and where service to others is encouraged.
- Sixth, a college or university is a celebrative community, one in which the heritage of the institution is remembered and where rituals affirming both tradition and change are widely shared [1990, pp. 7-8].

Struggling to nurture community in the culture of the academy is obviously hard work. By the very nature of our disciplines, the academy is built to recognize and honor different means of acquiring and recognizing truth. Yet strength of conviction on how we advance on the truth can be a fertile breeding ground for arrogance as well. And arrogance is an enemy of compassion.

Another principle of the academy is that we can hardly lay claim to the validity of an idea unless and until it has been tested against another. As John Stuart Mill notes, "He who knows only his own side of the case, knows little of that" (1956, p. 21). Thus, debate and dissent and other adversarial tools are central to collegiate culture. Our governance structures are not always well defined, the just-listed recommendation of the Carnegie report notwithstanding. These structures are loosely coupled combinations of hierarchial, collegial, and political systems, with overlays of symbolism. Thus, higher education governance can be a highly curious and puzzling matter. Decisions get made, and the work gets done. But if one tries to capture the flow of procedures and responsibilities, the tangled web of community and authority lines often defies rational and symbolic representation.

Other complications to the fulfillment of compassion in collegiate culture include the fact that the loyalties of scholars often lie outside the institution rather than inside. Recognition and reinforcement of scholarly work and worth also tend to lie beyond the perimeter of a campus. And in the forum of the university, we are constantly struggling with issues of equity—of gender, race, age, and sexual orientation—and with issues of public policy—abortion, school vouchers, women in combat military roles, AIDS, family values, revisionist history, and political correctness. These confront our nation and tax the goodwill and the community spirit of individuals within the academy. These matters touch every fiber of university operation, from personnel hiring and reward practices to the form and content of the curriculum.

We should not be surprised, then, that collegiate leaders have a first-class challenge in developing a sense of community. Of course, the balance of pluralism and community is not a leadership challenge restricted to the academy. A current movement that attempts to "balance the 'I' of individual rights with the 'we' of community needs" is the communitarian movement, headed by scholars such as Amitai Etzioni and Robert Bellah (Winkler, 1993, p. A12).

Etzioni's 1993 book, *The Spirit of Community,* and Bellah and others' earlier book, *Habits of the Heart,* both feature the challenge. According to Bellah, "We have committed what to the republican founders of our nation was the cardinal sin; we have put our own good, as individuals, as groups, ahead of the common good" (1985, p. 285).

And here is what Etzioni has to say in *The Spirit of Community:*

> From time to time there's a finding of social science that may by itself be of limited importance but illuminates a major conundrum: A study has shown that young Americans expect to be tried before a jury of their peers but are rather reluctant to serve on one. This paradox highlights a major aspect of contemporary American civic culture: a strong sense of entitlement—that is, a demand that the community provide more services and strongly uphold rights—coupled with a rather weak sense of obligation to the local and national community [p. 3].
>
> To take and not to give is an amoral, self centered predisposition that ultimately no society can tolerate. To revisit the finding that many try to evade serving on a jury, which, they claim, they have a right to be served by, is egotistical, indecent, and in the long run impractical. Hence, those most concerned about rights ought to be the first ones to argue for the resumption of responsibilities [p. 10].

The conversation has also found its way into public debate in other ways. A February 3, 1992, *Time* magazine article by Robert Hughes is entitled "The Fraying of America"; its subtitle reads, "When a Nation's Diversity Breaks into Factions, Demagogues Rush in, False Issues Cloud Debate, and Everybody Has a Grievance." Hughes writes, "America is a place filled with diversity, unsettled histories, images impinging on one another and spawning unexpected shapes. Its polyphony of voices, its constant eddying of claims to identify, is one of the things that make America. The gigantic, riven, hybridizing, multiracial republic each year receives a major share of the world's emigration, legal or illegal" (pp. 44, 46–47).

The respected American historian Arthur M. Schlesinger, Jr., has entered this debate in his 1992 book, *The Disuniting of America*. Schlesinger states, "The new ethnic gospel rejects the unifying vision of individuals from all nations melted into a new race. Its underlying philosophy is that America is not a nation of individuals at all, but a nation of groups. . . . Instead of a transformative nation with an identity all its own, America in this new light is seen as a preservative of diverse alien identities" (p. 16). In the academy and in the nation, then, the leadership question is whether we are a creation of common culture or a commonwealth of cultures. Perhaps in our civic and collegiate life we are a construction of both.

Now back to the academy. I have also been struck by the number of thoughtful pieces appearing on the theme of community in some of the premier higher education journals. Writing in the summer-fall 1989 issue of *Educational Record,* former Michigan State University president John Dibiaggio inquires about the president's role in the quality of campus life. He acknowledges that there is some debate about the extent to which the chief executive of a campus should attempt to shape and articulate its values: "I am equally convinced that a given college or university does have a distinct quality of life value system, and that each and every member of the campus community—the president included—must have a cultural appreciation for 'who we are'" (p. 10). Dibiaggio warns that there are two leadership dangers. The first is that a college president will be reluctant to advocate community values, and the other is that the president might be overprescriptive. The challenge of balance is part of the art form of leadership.

We have this view from the president's office on the nurture of community. Perhaps we should hear from the faculty. Jane Tompkins is a professor of English at a research university. In the November-December 1992 issue of *Change* magazine, she has contributed an article entitled "The Way We Live Now." The introduction to her article is a poignant statement of the challenge:

> I've come back from a walk down the corridors outside
> my university office. The halls are carpeted. The light-

ing is good. Secretaries in the main office occupy an attractive welcoming space. Individual offices have been redecorated within the recent past. Outside the windows, birds sing in the large green trees. It's a Wednesday afternoon in June, and I'm looking for someone to talk to. But, with only one exception, there are no professors in the offices I've walked by. The secretary I usually talk to has left for the day—she leaves early in the summer. Another is on leave of absence. A third is busy—I can hear her voice in the hall. So I walk back to my office, deflated. A momentary disappointment but the roots go deep. For some time now I've been restless and dissatisfied with my life the university, hungry for some emotional or spiritual fulfillment that it doesn't seem to afford. I crave a sense of belonging, the feeling that I'm part of an enterprise larger than myself, part of a group that shares some common purpose [p. 13].

How can collegiate leaders help nurture that common purpose? Those activities that involve the entire community in the review of mission and in the development of strategic plans surely offer the opportunity to pinpoint those values to which the larger university will give its allegiance. This is difficult work, and many academic groups will give up in frustration before they find the common ground. Yet the payoff is worth the investment. In the 1988 master plan for the university system of Florida, the nine-campus university and its governing board identified a cluster of fifteen values commitments. Among those are respect for the truth and love of learning, for the rights of others, and for other cultures and traditions (Florida Board of Regents, 1988). Compassion for others is also included in the list. The task of finding common values can be accomplished.

Moreover, college leaders have available the many opportunities of public utterance, of speeches and visits with groups within and without, to articulate the values of the community. More powerfully, however, these leaders can model these values in practice. I would encourage the reader to consider again some of the ideas offered in the dignity test of Chapter Two. When chairmen and chancellors, directors and deans, reflect civility in their behavior, we have a major contribution to community. And when faculty members are encouraged to salute the same value in their contact with students, community is likewise enhanced.

Hardly a day passes that does not offer some occasion for the cultivation of community and the active expression of compassion. A graduate student in a comprehensive university received a memo sent by a professor to all students in her graduate seminar. The memo expressed professorial disappointment to those students in the seminar who had not attended a recent visiting lecture. Apparently, the professor intended this event as a command performance. In military parlance, it means be there or else! The particular graduate student in question had a conflict with another course at the time the lecture was presented. However, she was offered no chance to explain to the professor and received the same "shotgun" memo as the others. This action was not a salute to dignity nor a contribution to community. Was this faculty member showing in her behavior the lessons she would like students to learn in their own teaching and careers? Instead, talk first, and write later. Do not launch written missiles at all targets when only a few are warranted. This is good advice for both faculty members and administrators.

A graduate student in psychology was trying to assemble her committee for the defense of her master's thesis. She was a student at an urban private university. Faculty members at this university were accustomed to arranging schedules for their convenience rather than that of students. They had classes on either Monday and Wednesday or Tuesday and Thursday. On those days when they had no classes, they were seen infrequently at the university, remaining ensconced in their suburban homes or away on consulting trips. The chairman of the psychology department left the graduate student to solve this scheduling puzzle (the chair's behavior was also a statement of university values) and made no attempt to help by insisting that one or more of the professors shift his or her campus schedule to attend the student's thesis defense. This was surely a behavioral expression of what the university and its faculty cared about. It is also surely one of the reasons that public trust in the university has been eroding.

Whether a college or university models the values it pro-
claims can be discerned informally, as in the previously cited illustrations, or more formally in a values audit, a process sponsored by
the Society for Values in Higher Education. And these values can
be discerned in other interesting ways.

In *Up the Organization* (1970), Robert Townsend recommends that executives try calling their own offices when they are
away from home to see what indignities have been built into their
organizations. What might people hear in such a call to the admissions office, the financial aid office, the vice president's or dean's
office? A cheerful and courteous voice with a service spirit asking
"How may I help you?" Or a crabby bureaucrat whose mission in
life is to irritate and frustrate saying "Whadda you want?" The
concept of a disguised observer is an interesting one and an instrument for keeping tabs on the values of our organizations. What
might we learn if we had a few of our students keep a semester's
journal on their best and "needs improvement" experiences with
the college or university?

A values audit? What applies to the collegiate organization
may apply to its leadership. A theme of this book is that the values
of the leader become explicit in his or her behavior and that our
colleagues constitute a staff auditing those values. Will our colleagues discern the presence and power of compassion in our daily
actions? A compassion for people, a compassion for community?
To these two, I add a compassion for standard and principle.

It is my intent to engage the concern for principle more
thoroughly in Chapter Seven. I would like to insert here, however,
a phrase used by Thomas Sergiovanni in *Moral Leadership* (1992).
He employs a useful phrase, "leadership by outrage," and he en-
larges on its meaning as follows: "Leadership by outrage, and the
practice of kindling outrage in others, challenges the conventional
wisdom that leaders should be poker-faced, play their cards close to
the chest, avoid emotion, and otherwise hide what they believe and
feel. When the source of leadership authority is moral, and when
covenants of shared values become the driving force for the school's
norm system, it seems natural to react with courage to shortcomings
in what we do and impediments to what we want to do" (p. 130).

Notice that Sergiovanni uses the word *courage,* an ideal to which we will turn in Chapter Six.

That a chair, dean, vice president, or president would not react with outrage to the aforementioned faculty behavior vis-à-vis the graduate student in psychology might be counted a notable disappointment—or even worse. For a collegiate leader not to express outrage at this neglect of the servant obligation must be counted an abdication of leadership responsibility.

And since I have already made some reference to Robert Townsend's irreverent but informing book *Up the Organization* (1970), I might as well suggest that universities could profit from the addition of a special kind of ombudsman suggested by Townsend: the vice president for antibureaucratization. Townsend recommends that the special responsibility for this vice president is to comb the organization for outmoded policies and foolish behaviors. Having spotted such a policy or behavior, the vice president takes position outside the office of the offending leader and yells "horseshit" at the top of his or her voice until the offending behavior ceases. A bit tongue-in-cheek and saucy for the hallowed halls of academe some might say. Actually, however, there is something to be said for a collegiate leader's assuming Townsend's proposed role occasionally and practicing leadership by outrage.

Leadership and Loving, Compassion and Courage

At the beginning of this chapter, I cited a number of works linking the words *leadership* and *love.* Let me repeat the exercise in these closing remarks. In his widely cited book *The Road Less Traveled,* author Scott Peck devotes one of his four major sections to the definition and meaning of love. Here is a key passage: "Love is not simply giving; it is judicious giving and judicious withholding as well. It is judicious praising and judicious criticizing. It is judicious arguing, struggling, confronting, urging, pushing, and pulling in addition to comforting. *It is leadership*" (1978, p. 111, my emphasis). This is an interesting circular venture. I have defined leadership in part as an act of love. Peck defines love as an act of leadership. The capacity for both love and leadership, it strikes me, is encouraged and enlarged via a journey in which we experience not achievement but failure, not satisfaction but disappointment, not pleasure but pain, not the easy decisions of clearly right and clearly wrong but those wrenching ones that transport us into the night of soul and spirit, where we wrestle with dilemma and complexity and rid our personalities of sterility and rigidity and the need for perfection. And we emerge from the journey with a strengthened inclination for caring and a more authentic capacity for it.

As earlier noted, I have vacationed with my family a few days each summer on Hilton Head Island. Among the visual memories of the island I have stored in mind is a solitary giant oak tree a short walk from the Atlantic beach. This is not a stately and dignified oak, not a tree whose massive limbs reach in natural yearning for the sky. It is a gnarled and twisted oak, whose great limbs have been contorted by some earlier and unknown force of nature and now reach out in awkward angle from its base, running low to the ground and then turning upward. One cannot pass this tree without pausing and reflecting on what history and botanical pain are represented in those limbs. The more regular and stately giant oaks are beautiful. But this special oak arrests one's attention and invites admiration as one considers that it survived those forces that caused hurt and disfiguration, transforming those forces into a victory and standing transfixed now in a forest statue, a living and commanding memorial representing the translation of stress into strength. And so too are the possibilities in our journeys of learning and loving. Leadership compassion is more likely to be nurtured in the difficult moments of our journey, and then we may be able to give the gift of compassion more surely.

Alan Paton, the South African writer and author of *Cry, the Beloved Country,* wrote a beautiful piece called "The Challenge of Fear," appearing in the 1968 collection of essays *What I Have Learned.* In his essay, Paton observes that we often consider courage as the opposite of fear but "in the dynamic sense the opposite of fear is love, whether this be love of man or love of justice" (p. 254). A few pages later, Paton concludes, "Active loving saves one from a morbid preoccupation with the shortcomings of society and the waywardness of men" (p. 257).

I use these reflections on compassion as both end and beginning. An active compassion is an essential ideal of effective leadership. I have tried in these musings to reveal how and why collegiate leaders should invest their behavior with compassion for both people and principle, a love of person and of justice. At the same time, this caring in some ways becomes the foundation for the exercise of courage, which is the topic of our next chapter. In that chapter, we will explore not so much the physical aspects of courage; rather, we will visit courage as the natural outgrowth of caring. Let us turn, then, to an ideal that flows from compassion.

6

The Question of Courage

I ended Chapter Five on the note that courage is a natural out-growth of caring. What thoughts come to mind when we hear that word *courage*? Perhaps we will recall from memory some historic event—Xenophon and the ten thousand and their heroic guard of the Greek retreat, David confronting Goliath or Queen Esther confronting Haman, Florence Nightingale in the Crimea, General McAuliffe responding "Nuts!" to the German request for surrender at the Battle of the Bulge in World War II, Martin Luther King leading the struggle for civil rights.

But there are other heroes and quieter expressions of courage. In *Some Do Care* (1992), Anne Colby and William Damon offer an interesting insight into the nature of moral courage as they profile in their book a few (twenty-three) quiet and little-known moral exemplars in our society today. Suzie Valdez is known as the "Queen of the Dump" in Ciudad Juárez, Mexico. When her husband left her in California, Suzie moved with her four children to El Paso, Texas, where she took on the personal mission of feeding and clothing the children living in and around the garbage dump in Ciudad Juárez. When she made that move to Texas from California, she was a single mother with four children, no car, a tenth-grade education, only a slight knowledge of Spanish, no work experience, and no money. She had only the mission in mind, one driven by her religious faith. This is not leadership by virtue of position but leadership by virtue of passion.

Later in the book, Colby and Damon profile a woman from a different heritage. Virginia Durr came from an aristocratic southern family. She was well educated and her husband a Rhodes Scholar. Virginia Durr invested her adult life as a champion of justice and equity; she focused especially on the impediments to justice and equity for black men and women in the South. "Virginia Foster Durr spent over thirty years leading the struggle to outlaw the poll tax, which had been used for many years to prevent women, blacks, and poor people from voting" (p. 95).

At the beginning of their study of moral exemplars, Colby and Damon pose questions that are certainly pertinent to our inquiry in this chapter: "How is it that some people are drawn over and over again to acts that serve others rather than only themselves? How do certain people muster the courage to stick by their principles when under enormous pressure to abandon them? How can such people maintain their integrity in the face of endless temptations to compromise it?" (p. 3).

One of the findings that emerged from Colby and Damon's study was that the question of courage was rarely reflected on by these leaders. They were so consumed by the moral principle at hand that little thought was given to their own bravery. The authors comment on two contemporary moral exemplars: "Like all the exemplars in this book, Sakharov and Gandhi subjected themselves to great risks. It is noteworthy that, in his memoirs, Sakharov seldom (if ever) remarks on his own moral courage. It is as if he assumes that he has no choice in matters of principle. Courage seems moot, even necessary, in such a light. This, too, is a pattern that we observed in our twenty-three exemplars." (p. 16).

Do I need to rethink and retitle this chapter? Might it be more accurate to say that leaders do not think about courage but about principle? Might it be true that the absence of courage is simply an absence of caring, a condition of moral bankruptcy?

Courage is a critical design ideal for effective leadership. Some might suggest that courage is the ability to appear outwardly composed and confident when you are inwardly racked with fear and anxiety. There are other expressions of courage. There is the courage to discharge one's acknowledged duty, the courage to endure and persist, the courage to accept and affirm one's sense of self, and the courage to reach and risk.

The Courage to Do Our Duty

In a collection of essays entitled *Moral Principles in Education*, John Dewey explores the meaning and development of moral character. He asserts, "The consciousness of ends must be more than merely intellectual. We can imagine a person with most excellent judgment, yet who does not act upon his judgment" (1975, p. 52). Dewey notes earlier that "the individual must have the power to stand up and count for something in the actual conflicts of life" (p. 50). It is action that infuses our design ideals with meaning and power. A first expression of courage is the strength to stand to one's duty.

What should we say about this word *duty?* Duty is the work of putting one foot in front of the other day after day, honestly and faithfully discharging leadership responsibilities. Duty implies that we are willing to face our responsibilities on those days when we are targeted and tired as well as those days when we are filled when energy and cheer. Duty implies that we are willing to do our work when frustration and failure thwart our efforts as well as on those days when achievement and accomplishment furnish elevating moments. Duty implies that we set heart and mind to task when we stand alone as well as when we ride a wave of popularity. Duty implies that we stand to the task when moments of uncertainty and ambiguity afflict our spirit as well as when the path seems clear and confidence is high.

Duty is not always a colorful and dashing matter but is often a grit-your-teeth-and-carry-on affair. I think of a friend who has been serving as a vice president of finance and administration in a research university for over a decade. In that time, his institution has experienced budget cuts for eight of the ten years, and the institution has raised fees eight of those years. He has labored with a massive physical plant desperately in need of refurbishing and with maintenance equipment woefully out of date (they are still carrying a 1948 Dodge truck on the active equipment inventory). If we caught him at the right moment on any given day, we might find his jaw dragging on the floor. But at most moments and with most colleagues, he conveys an unfailing optimism, a can-do attitude. Nor has he let his imagination and invention atrophy. His initiative has been chiefly responsible for the development of an important new power generation facility that will save the university large sums in its utility budget and will actually result in additional income through a cogeneration arrangement.

At a time when many faculty and staff members of the university have departed for other states because of the miserable financial climate, this man has continued to invest his talent in the life of the university. Indeed, the long years of financial difficulty have had their impact on his personal welfare. In length of service, he is easily the most experienced of the vice presidents at this university. Yet at one time, he was earning less than all of his colleagues because of salary compression problems occasioned by more recently appointed vice presidents coming into the institution at market salaries. Even this indignity has not taken from him the power of a resilient spirit. He will retire in a few years, having given over thirty years to this university. This is a quiet and relatively unheralded story. The most he might expect in the way of public recognition for his attention to duty will be a resolution of appreciation from the institution's governing board. In his heart, however, he will carry his own medal of honor.

This friend has also stood to his duty in other ways. At one time, one of his unit directors was found to be abusing the privilege of office (as discovered in an internal audit). The unit director was a member of a minority, a close friend and confidant of many minority leaders in the community. Relieving this director raised the possibility of community conflict surrounding the university at a time when it was working hard to increase the number of minority faculty and staff members and students.

Long a champion of opportunity (the original appointment of this director being one among many evidences of his commitment), this vice president steadfastly held to his conviction that the expectation of performance and integrity would be honored without regard to race or gender among his staff. And so he did his duty and terminated the employment of the director in a decisive but quiet act. The style with which he approached this delicate personnel decision revealed his commitment to another governing ideal of this book, that of dignity.

I think of another executive responsible for a system that has recently sustained dramatic budget cuts. She is a collegiate leader who possessed that "most excellent judgment" to which Dewey refers in his essays. She has had the strength of character to translate her judgments into actions, actions that maintained the integrity and community of a system that might have spun into disorder and depression. With courage and competence, she has done her duty.

Duty, honor, country: these are words recognized by all military leaders in our nation. In his farewell address before the cadets at West Point on May 16, 1962, General of the Army Douglas MacArthur uttered these extemporary remarks that were later recorded in his autobiography, *Reminiscences:*

> Duty-Honor-Country. Those three hallowed words reverently dictate what you ought to be, what you can be, what you will be. . . . They teach you to be proud and unbending in honest failure, but humble and gentle in success, not to substitute words for actions, not to seek the path of comfort, but to face the stress and spur of difficulty and challenge; to learn to stand up in the storm but to have compassion on those who fail; to master yourself before you seek to master others; to have a heart that is clean, a goal that is high; to learn to laugh yet never forget how to weep; to reach into the future, yet never neglect the past; to be serious yet never to take yourself too seriously; to be modest so that you will remember the simplicity of true greatness, the open mind of true wisdom, the meekness of true strength. They give you a temper of the will, a quality of the imagination, a vigor of the emotions, a freshness of the deep springs of life, a temperamental predominance of courage over timidity, an appetite for adventure over ease. They create in your heart the sense of wonder, the unfailing hope of

what next, and the joy and inspiration of life [1964, pp. 423-424].

Here was a leader pulled from retirement to lead the military forces of this nation in two additional conflicts. He took that leadership at a moment of defeat and helped fashion not only the architecture of victory in the Pacific in World War II but the architecture of recovery for Japan. His words and his actions are splendid operational expressions of the courage to do our duty. This was work not of the moment but of the years, work also representing another face of courage: that to endure and persist.

The Courage to Endure and Persist

In their book *Leaders: The Strategies for Taking Charge,* Warren Bennis and Burt Nanus attribute the following statement to Ray Kroc, the former president and founder of McDonald's restaurants: "Nothing in the world can take the place of persistence. Talent will not; nothing is more common than unsuccessful men with great talent. Genius will not; unrewarded genius is almost a proverb. Education will not; the world is full of educated derelicts. Persistence, determination alone are omnipotent" (1985, p. 45). Bennis and Nanus also quote Admiral Hyman Rickover on the importance of staying the course: "Good ideas are not adopted automatically. They must be driven into practice with courageous patience" (p. 43). I like the phrase "courageous patience."

We live in an "instant world"; our expectation is that we can mix most any substance with a little water, put it in the microwave, and have the finished product in a moment or two. We may have lost the patience of the craftsman, whose vision unfolds by the careful hand, by a devoted and stalwart spirit employed over time. In *No Easy Victories* (1968), John Gardner notes, "Ours is a difficult and exhilarating form of government—not for the faint of heart, not for the tidy-minded, and in these days of complexity not for the stupid. We need men and women who can bring to government the highest order of intellect, social motivations sturdy enough to pursue good purposes despite setbacks, and a resilience of spirit equal to the frustrations of public life" (p. 6). Let me recall the two biographical notes on Suzie Valdez and Virginia Durr, the two moral exemplars we cited from *Some Do Care*. In each case, the leadership investment of these two women reached over a lifetime. The passion for dignity and for justice commanded a life's work. They had the courage to persist.

In the life of colleges and universities, the effective leader realizes from the beginning that these are institutions whose mission and construction are not built to accommodate rapid change. The leader who hopes to dash in for a quick fix may see that quick fix fade as quickly. When one looks at the growth and achievement of any college or university, one realizes that these achievements are the result of patient and skillful bricklaying. And for the most part, the bricklaying is done by those artisans of thought and action who make long-term investments in the institution and not those who flit from one place to another serving their own ambition. If I might recall a phrase earlier cited, the men and women who build our colleges and universities for the long run are artisans of both vision and will.

Here I would like to pause for a brief excursion on ambition. An interesting little book nestled in the bookshelves of my office is a 1980 volume by Joseph Epstein called *Ambition: The Secret Passion*. His opening pages introduce us to the difficulties of thinking about the value and role of ambition: "One can, after all, be ambitious for the public good, for the alleviation of suffering, for the enlightenment of mankind, though there are some who say that these are precisely the ambitious people most to be mistrusted. Yet, if a brief definition is needed, I should define ambition as the fuel of achievement" (p. 1). I would not want to quarrel with Epstein's definition, but I would invite reflection on the instrumentality suggested in his note. An ambition to serve others may be usefully distinguished from an ambition to serve self. In the pages of the *Chronicle of Higher Education,* one can read interesting stories of presidents who have been in office fewer than two or three years before becoming candidates for other positions. When former Florida State president Dale Lick looked at the presidency at Michigan State University before his chair was warm at Florida State, he was invited to vacate that presidential chair (Leatherman, 1993, p. A21). According to the story, Lick also had not bothered to advise his boss, board of regents chancellor Charles Reed, that he was a candidate at MSU.

In Chapter One, I began this book with the observation that some presidents and collegiate leaders are architects of their own difficulty or demise. The call of power, prestige, and pay has unhinged the judgment of many an academic leader and caused an imbalance in the legitimate instrument of ambition. Who would want to have as a leadership colleague one who did not care enough for his or her previous work to have made a sustained and serious investment in the mission and people of that place, a servant of self rather than others? This is a question that we will reconsider in Chapter Eight. Now back to the constructive force of persistence.

One can find lovely stories of devotion and persistence throughout the pages of literature and biography. One among a thousand such examples is *To Serve Them All My Days* (1972), R. F. Delderfield's fictional account of an English headmaster who devoted his entire life to a school and its pupils. It is a tale without grand sweep of place and time and actors, one of simple devotion to cause. In this novel, Headmaster David Powlett-Jones teaches his young English pupils the same values and virtues, the uses of courage and caring, that we so desire to find and encourage among collegiate leaders today.

Since we spoke of bricklaying previously, I also like two verses taken from the Old Testament book of Nehemiah. Nehemiah records his work in rebuilding the walls of Jerusalem as follows: "So we built the wall; and all the wall was joined together unto the half thereof; for the people had a mind to work" (Nehemiah 4:3). And when his enemies and detractors would detain him from the work of rebuilding the wall, Nehemiah records, "And I sent messengers unto them, saying, I am doing a great work, so that I cannot come down; why should the work cease, whilst I leave it, and come down to you?" (Nehemiah 6:3). This is a record of persistent leadership.

Of the pleasures I recall from my own administrative adventures, few took form in the short time frame of days and months; their gestation period involved several years. The design and implementation of a new registration system at Memphis State University in the mid sixties, of the performance incentive policy for Tennessee higher education in the mid to late seventies, and of a National Collegiate Athletic Association (NCAA) Division III intercollegiate program at LSU Shreveport (about which more later) all required many years of effort, as did the building of the Noel Memorial Library there in the eighties.

When I first went to LSU Shreveport, the campus had a strong intramural program but no intercollegiate athletic one. There were many individuals on the faculty and staff who strongly resisted an intercollegiate program; they believed that it would damage the strong academic reputation of the university, a reputation that had been patiently earned over a period of years. Indeed, in my first year, 1980, I maintained a healthy skepticism about the proper approach. A faculty and staff task force recommended that we develop an intercollegiate athletic program, but this recommendation came at a moment when the university began to experience the first of several consecutive years of budget cuts, so we placed the proposal temporarily on the back burner.

As I continued to fret about the matter, however, I became more and more convinced that the implementation of a nonscholarship intercollegiate athletic program would be entirely within the spirit of the university, would enhance its emotional center, would help foster a keener sense of community, would help strengthen the bonds between campus and community, and would furnish another instrument of learning for some of our students. Moreover, I felt that the university would be giving an important signal of leadership to emphasize the NCAA Division III level of competition. This level was rarely found among public institutions in the South, as most seemed intent in trying to break into the big time in Division I competition. My hope was that perhaps LSU Shreveport's entry into Division III or the National Association of Intercollegiate Athletics (NAIA) might call some other institutions to that flag. At the same time, I realized that the campus would face inevitable tensions and temptations to escalate its program to another level.

I had pledged to the faculty that we would not implement the athletic program unless and until the students were willing to approve a small student fee to support the program. The faculty nevertheless defeated the proposal; many people believed, perhaps correctly, that it was folly to begin an intercollegiate program when our finances were such that we could hardly afford resources for the library and other academic needs. Perhaps I could have persuaded the LSU Board to approve the program, even in the face of this vote, but I wanted the university community, faculty and students, to own the program. It was now 1986, six years into my ten-year investment as chancellor.

In the fall of 1989, I took the proposal back to the faculty senate where this time it was approved unanimously. And to make sure we had faculty support, I asked that the senate vote be reviewed by the entire faculty of the university, where the proposal was again approved by a commanding majority of the faculty. To this day, I am not sure what happened in the intervening three years that made the difference in the vote. Perhaps giving the proposal time to move among faculty members, to avoid the idea that it was being rammed home. Perhaps the faculty became convinced, as I had, not only that was this a good thing for our students but that it might help strengthen our competitive posture for enrollments, so that nobility and philosophy were married to self-interest and practicality.

I do remember quite distinctly, however, walking back across campus on that fall afternoon of 1989 with several members of the faculty. One among them was Dr. Ann Torrans, a longtime and splendid member of the faculty. Ann was known both for her investment of time and talent in the university and for her outspoken advocacy of causes she championed and her tenacious resistance to those she did not.

Ann turned to me and said, "Chancellor, do you know why I voted for that athletic program today?"

I responded, "Well, Ann, I hope that you voted for the proposal because you thought it was the right thing for us to do."

"No," she quipped, "I voted for it because I knew that you were going to continue bringing it back to the faculty until we did finally pass it."

Well, we enjoyed a few light moments over this exchange. And we began play in the spring of 1990 in tennis and soccer, moving to basketball and baseball in 1990–91. I am now chancellor emeritus, but the intercollegiate athletic program is there and according to reports it is thriving. I would like to think the program

exists because perseverance gave us time to develop the allegiance
and ownership of the faculty, the staff, and the students.

There are other stories of persistence, stories of campuses
struggling to maintain historic missions in the face of financial and
educational pressures to change. I think, for example, of Mills College in California, a private college for women, endeavoring to keep
its mission and role while many other former women's colleges have
made the transition to coed enrollments. And I think of Fisk College
in Tennessee, a private historically black college, grappling with
financial hardship. Written in the histories of these two campuses
and a hundred others are stories of the courage to persist.

The Courage to Reach and Risk

In his inspiring book *A Touch of Wonder*, Arthur Gordon quotes
advice given to him: "Love life. Be grateful for it always. And show
your gratitude by not shying away from its challenges. Try always
to live a little bit beyond your capacities. You'll find that you never
succeed" (1974, p. 206). This note concludes a quick chapter entitled
simply "Be Bold," in which Gordon celebrates the virtue of risk
taking and boldness; he reminds us that a willingness to extend our
reach, to try new ventures, will often help us discover reservoirs of
ability that might have remained latent without the challenge.

This call to boldness does not imply foolishness. It is a call
to challenge our ability and our emotions, to manifest curiosity, as
I noted in Chapter Three. Every leader faces his or her own Goli-
aths, formidable foes whose size and strength appear overwhelming
and strike fear in our hearts. If we are not courageous, our fear will
clothe itself in reality. But courage also may clothe itself in reality:
"he has not learned the lesson of life who does not every day sur-
mount a fear" is the advice of Emerson, who comments further on
the nature of courage: "The third excellence is courage, the perfect
will, which no terrors can shake, which is attracted by frowns or
threats or hostile armies, nay, needs these to awake and fan its
reserved energies into a pure flame, and is never quite itself until
the hazard is extreme; then it is serene and fertile, and all its powers
play well" (1929, p. 697).

Courage is an instrument of discovery, a self-reinforcing

journey that begets confidence, which in turn enables courage. Neither confidence nor courage is nurtured in activities of safe industry and investment. The terrors of the darkness fade and vanish with the sunlight of courage. Courage simply reveals that a leader loves and honors a point of principle, what is right, above all else. Courage, then, is a measure of our devotion to principle.

Nor is the call to courage a call to be without fear. The presence of courage does not denote the absence of fear and anxiety. Corporate or collegiate, any leader who claims that she or he has never experienced cold sweats and moist palms in facing some challenge is failing the candor test.

On January 2, 1989, I prepared to drive onto the campus of LSU Baton Rouge to take on responsibilities as interim chancellor there, a change in assignment noted earlier. After a few moments of revving the car's engine and psyching up my own mental and emotional one, I decided that the cold feeling in the pit of my stomach was not going to disappear. So I pulled out the sound-track tape from *Superman,* shoved it in the tape player, turned up the volume, and went driving on to campus as though I belonged there and knew what I was doing. I had a lot of fun during those few months, moments of pleasure and memories of splendid colleagues that remain to this day. These moments and memories I could not have experienced so vividly without that initial moment of anxiety.

There are different challenges for each personality and talent. The leader who can address an audience of a thousand with confidence may be someone unable to confront a single colleague with bad news without heart palpitations. The leader who is comfortable and confident among political and civic leaders in the hallways of power may be an individual whose insides quiver as he or she appears before a meeting of the faculty. Emerson phrases the contrast quite beautifully: "There is a courage of the cabinet as well as courage of the field; a courage of manners in private assemblies; and another in public assemblies; a courage which enables one man to speak masterly to a hostile company, whilst another man who can easily face a cannon's mouth dares not open his own" (1929, p. 702).

I am thinking about two college presidents. One of these was a former defensive back on the football field who had discovered that momentum was a determining factor in bringing down an

opposing running back and who had developed a fierce reputation
for "ringing the bell" of offensive players who found themselves
traversing his field of play. Yet this same president could never
bring himself to deal personally and directly with difficult situations where a colleague needed either correction or containment.
The courage of the field did not transfer to his office.

Another president was invested with modest physique and
only sandlot experience in sport. Erring and duplicitous colleagues
discovered, however, that this president lacked neither caring nor
courage in his interpersonal relations. Those who were trying for
a good work met with reinforcing affection. Those who trod a
shoddy or dishonest path encountered a lively and effective shift in
leadership style; they also found that the avoidance of pain can
sometimes become a source of intense and useful motivation.

Affirming the theme of diverse expressions of courage is Mir-
iam Polster's book *Eve's Daughters* (1992). She calls our attention
to stylistic differences in the heroic traits of men and women and
offers thoughtful portraits that emphasize the many ways in which
courage is expressed: "Nien Cheng, for example, stubbornly refused
to 'confess' to sins against the Communist regime in China and
eventually outlasted her interrogators. Her imprisonment, which
achieved nothing for her captors, finally became an embarrassment
to them. . . . Harriet Tubman is an excellent representative of the
magnetism of kinship. She has been called the Moses of her people
for bringing them out of slavery" (pp. 32-33). These and other
examples enlarge our sense of what it means to be courageous.

Now let me tie these explorations of the different faces and
forms of courage back to the theme of this discussion, the courage
to reach and risk. In *Women of Influence, Women of Vision* (1991),
Astin and Leland make clear that risk taking was an important
characteristic of that group of women leaders they identified as
instigators. The courage to dare, to risk, has never been a macho and
male quality only. Nor is it an ostentatious one. True courage, as
we have noted throughout this chapter, is often a quiet exercise of
the will and at the more visible level is seen as a passionate commitment to principles of moral posture such as justice, equity, dignity. Boldness is not the same as loudness.

This face and form of leader courage suggest two things. Not only does the leader care for principle, exhibiting a commanding passion for justice, equity, dignity, but he or she is also willing to discover the power of extending beyond personal experience and current ability levels as a means of developing and nurturing the best that is within. In *Essays, Civil and Moral,* Sir Francis Bacon offers this note: "Illi mors gavis incubat, qui notus nimis omnibus, ignotus moritur sibi" [It is a sad fate for a man to die too well known to everybody else, and still unknown to himself] (1937, p. 29). This nugget of advice allies nicely with that of MacArthur, earlier cited, to master ourselves before we seek to master others. Neither self-knowledge nor self-mastery, however, are goals that leaders are likely to realize without the ideal of courage.

The Courage to Affirm Self

In *The Many Lives of Academic Presidents,* Clark Kerr and Marian Gade (1986) illuminate the diversity of settings and personalities in the college presidency. In the prestigious Ivy League university, the dilapidated slum school building housing a community college, and the nontraditional college located in a former mortuary are found the equally varied men and women who serve as college presidents. There are the 30-year-old whiz kid with a divinity doctorate who has taken over the reins at a private college, the executive in his late forties (without doctorate) from industry in his fifth year as president of a public university, the bearded sixty-year-old engineering Ph.D. in his third year as president of a research university, and the energetic and poised Ed.D. fresh from a dean's appointment who has become the first woman president in a state university system. The journey for each of these diverse leaders will have followed a different terrain. And what is true for college presidents will be equally true for vice presidents, deans, and directors. We would wish that these individual journeys have been ones of self-discovery.

A few years ago I gave a speech called "The Flogging of Theagenes" (1984), delivered to a civic audience when I was chancellor at LSU Shreveport. The title of the speech was derived from the story of a famous Greek athlete of 500 B.C. The many prizes won by Theagenes during his athletic career moved the citizens of Thasus to erect a statue in his honor. The story is told that one of his detractors came each evening to flog the statue of Theagenes, this behavior apparently flowing from a deeply harbored jealousy. The nightly flogging continued until one evening the statue of Theagenes fell on the detractor and killed him.

Now that is the origin of the title. The theme of the speech centered on the destructive forces of imitation and jealousy, the sad record of leaders (can we call them that?) throwing themselves against the personality and performance of others rather than discovering the power and promise of their own personality. Effective leaders have a strong sense of personal identity and resist the idea that they can be, or should be, all things to all people. This affirmation of self, this sense of autonomy prevents them from being swayed by the expectations of others and allows them to be authentic in their relationships. As Abraham Zaleznik notes, "This active location and placement of one's self prevents the individual from being defined by others in uncongenial terms" (1966, pp. 41-42). The leader who has the courage to affirm self is one who

- Recognizes that there is a thin line between arrogance and confidence
- Knows how to express compassion within the special capacity of his or her personality
- Understands how to distinguish between role and self
- Realizes that imitation and phoniness are destructive of leadership effectiveness
- Appreciates that spontaneous expressions of conviction give colleagues a more accurate glimpse into our real selves
- Recognizes that perfection, the absence of error and mistake, is an unlikely condition for leaders who are interested in learning and achieving
- Knows how to be gracious in receiving and rejecting criticism
- Understands how to rejoice in those special attributes that define the uniqueness and boundaries of self

The opportunity to both discover and affirm self will not always await the special strength that can come from years of experience but may arrive at earlier and expected moments in the lives of collegiate leaders. Hence, exploring our design ideals at every moment in our careers is important.

Wellesley president Diana Walsh had been in office less than three months when confronted by a complex issue on her campus. She publicly denounced a book published by one of her own faculty members. *The Jewish Onslaught: Dispatches from the Wellesley Battlefront,* by Tony Martin, a professor of Africana Studies at Wellesley, attacks faculty and students at Wellesley, both Jewish and black. In a letter to students, the faculty, and alumnae, President Walsh comments, "We are profoundly disturbed and saddened by Professor Martin's new book because it gratuitously attacks individuals and groups at Wellesley College through innuendo and the application of racial and religious stereotype" (Magner, 1994, p. 12). President Walsh later defended Professor Martin's academic freedom to offer the views expressed in his book. Here is a tangled ethical web that would test the judgment and the courage of any collegiate leader. In this case, very early in her tenure, President Walsh faced a test that gave her national visibility and an opportunity to explore the meaning of courage.

President Walsh will understand the meaning of a passage nestled in the middle of Hugh Prather's conversational little book *Notes on Love and Courage:* "Pain must never be taken philosophically; otherwise it isn't pain, we haven't yet opened up. The more human we become the more likely we are to suffer. Approachable means vulnerable, woundable, not made hard by a history of abuse, but like old leather, made softer, more comfortable to be near" (1977).

Reframing the Question—A Summary

The title for this chapter is "The Question of Courage." Perhaps, however, I should reframe the inquiry. The evidence suggests that effective leaders spend little time in thinking of their courage or proving it. In some ways, the question of leader courage may not be the best or correct one. A better question for those who aspire to lead is "Do I care enough to do the right thing?" Indeed, we might also compress the many definitions of leaders into the simple proposition that they are moral exemplars.

The presence of courage in the lives of such leaders, our moral exemplars, is attested by operational evidence. The collegiate administrator willing to risk and dare, to experience isolation and solitude, to employ a standard other than popularity and accolade, to confront wrongdoing, to maintain integrity in the face of temptation, to act when faced with the agony of ethical uncertainty—this is a leader of courage. The man or woman who stands to duty, faithfully discharging his or her responsibilities in good times and bad—this is a leader of courage. The colleague who endures and persists, who invests her or his life for the long run—this is a leader of courage. That friend who continues to reach and to risk, to venture outside the bounds of safety and security—this is a leader of courage. An associate who can affirm the best in his or her personality while working to improve is a courageous leader. The collegiate administrator who absorbs, endures, and conquers the enmity of those mired in tradition and convention in order to know the joy of creation—this is also a leader of courage.

Such moral exemplars evidence in their lives a quiet but persistent passion for basic virtues, a passion for principle—for justice, dignity, and equity. And they are exemplars of yet another design ideal to which we turn in Chapter Seven—the ideal of excellence.

7

The Expectation of Excellence

There are moments of epiphany in each of our lives that cause us to understand more fully the meaning of the word *excellence*. There are other moments that might be described not so much as those of an epiphany as those of moderate professional terror—but with the promise of excellence residing even there. Several years ago, the visual arts community of Shreveport decided to conduct the Beaux Arts Brush Off. Several prominent citizens from over the city were invited to be artists for a day. Their palette productions would be sold at a black-tie auction, and the proceeds would be used in supporting local art galleries. The entire top floor of the largest bank building in town was reserved for the event. The idea was that these civic leaders would arrive in smock and beret to give birth to their paintings, changing later into tux for the auction. As chancellor of LSU Shreveport, I was among those identified for this event.

It is difficult to appreciate the anxiety this civic call created in my life. Recall, please, the remarks of Emerson concerning varieties of courage from Chapter Six. I can give speeches in civic and professional settings large and small, usually with no fright beyond that initial moment of anxiety that even the most seasoned speakers might experience before an address. But I can barely draw a straight line and have absolutely no talent for painting, or at least that I have ever discovered. I suffered a private terror. My vision of this event was that it was destined to be a moment of public humiliation for me, for my family, and for the university. I lay awake nights thinking of how I would be frozen before my canvas, while the rich and famous of the community looked on to increase my discomfort, waiting for the first strokes to appear.

What to paint? What to paint? Why did they not ask me to play the French horn? I could manage a few decent notes on that instrument, residuals from earlier mastery and performance history in college orchestra and later in three city symphonies. Finally, one morning I popped awake with solution in mind. I went over to the art supply store and purchased two tubes of paint, a parchment brown and a black, and I equipped myself with two brushes, one of broad stroke and one of fine stroke. On the night of the event, I confidently donned smock and beret, looked lovingly at my wife dressed in a sophisticated blue silk dress, and assured her that she would not be embarrassed during the evening. When we arrived at the "artists loft" in the bank building, I set about my work. First, I painted the entire canvas with the parchment brown, to simulate a piece of musical composition paper. I painted a musical staff on this background and then the notes for the first four measures of a composition for French horn that I had framed in my mind earlier to be entitled "Villanelle," a dance for horn in F.

It was a primitive work. A lovely woman of the city named Carolyn Nelson bought the painting at auction for $250, as I recall. She will always occupy a special place of affection in my memories. And she has in her home what can euphemistically be described as an original and one-of-a-kind art piece. There is a relevant line in Kahlil Gibran's beautiful book *Sand and Foam,* "It is only when we are pursued that we become swift" (1973, p. 79). Imagination can be stoked by fear. Whether imagination leads to excellence in every case may be debated. We can stimulate excellence by pulling with our expectancy or pursuing with our expectancy.

There is a circle of promise around every individual and organization, a circle representing the idea of excellence possible for each. Whether we and our colleagues, our organizations, and their clients experience the promise of excellence may depend on the energizing effect of leader expectations.

The Nurture of Personal Excellence

If we wonder if we are in need of leadership to advance the idea of personal excellence in our society and our colleges and universities today, any reading of our morning newspaper or a weekly reading of the *Chronicle of Higher Education* would erase the doubt.

On this point, I find the writing of Etzioni compelling, as he observes in his book *The Spirit of Community:*

> The moral condition of other areas is similarly a source of concern. Almost half of Americans surveyed report chronic malingering at work and calling in sick when they are not sick; one sixth admit that they have abused drugs or alcohol while at work. Six of ten (59 percent) admit to have used physical force against another person—and fewer than half (45 percent) regret it. Twenty five percent of Americans say they would abandon their families for money, and 7 percent admit freely that they would kill someone if paid enough. The moral patrimony of the eighties has been the proliferation of cost-benefit analysis into realms in which it has no place; it has devalued matters such as life, companionship, and integrity that ought not to be subject to such superficial quantification [1993, p. 27].

Today, as yesterday, our schools and colleges have a commanding challenge in moral education, which is intimately and directly connected to the idea of excellence. No writer has delivered a more stimulating and informing treatise on this theme than John Gardner in his well-known book *Excellence*. He emphasizes the delicate role that education plays in the identification and the development of human talent. His book should be read by every educational leader; its price is justified by these lines alone: "But excellence implies more than competence. It implies striving for the highest standards in every phase of life. . . . We are beginning to understand that free men must set their own difficult goals and be their own hard taskmasters. . . . They must cherish what Whitehead called the 'habitual habit of greatness.' " (1984, pp. 160–161).

In *The Fifth Discipline* (1990), Peter Senge offers this conviction: "I do not believe great organizations have ever been built by trying to emulate one another, any more than individual greatness is achieved by trying to copy another 'great person' " (p. 11). Under this assumption, excellence results not from imitating another institution or individual but from reaching for and discovering one's own promise and distinction, whether personal or organizational. This is an idea reminiscent of Gardner and an earlier American scholar, Emerson:

> There is a time in every man's education when he arrives at the conviction that envy is ignorance; that imitation is suicide; that he must take himself for better or worse as his portion. The power that resides in him is new in nature, and none but he knows what that is which he can do, nor does he know until he has tried [1929, p. 139].
>
> Insist on yourself; never imitate. Your own gift you can present every moment with the cumulative force of a whole life's cultivation; but of the adopted talent of another you have only extemporaneous half possession [1929, p. 150].

It seems to me that the nurture of personal excellence, in our lives and in those of our colleagues and clients, resides in these principles, which involve

- A respect for variety of talent and the excellence promised in each talent
- A respect for the power of encouragement and expectancy in causing each talent to reach the outer circle of its promise
- A respect for the test of performance rather than pedigree as the appropriate test of excellence
- A respect for the formative role of education—of ideas and skill, of discipline and daring, of practice and persistence—in the development of talent

- A respect for standards of performance that call us to stand on our mental, emotional, and physical tiptoes
- A respect for pride of craftsmanship, a nurture and celebration of the urge to do our best in whatever task or challenge set before us

A newly appointed president tells of an excellence test in her first week on the job. The Department of Health, Physical Education and Recreation had occupied an impressive new building. From the faculty and departmental perspective, an obvious next step was to propose the implementation of a new master's degree program. The proposal arrived on the president's desk, who was expected to forward it with her blessing to the institution's governing board and, assuming favorable review, to the state coordinating board.

Carrying a relatively undistinguished curriculum outline, the proposed program offered no promise of distinction in either mission or delivery from other programs already available in the region. Nor could any evidence of need be found anywhere in the proposal—no surveys of recent graduates, no citation of appropriate manpower statistics, no commentary from possible employers of graduates, such as schools, the recreation industry, and so forth. Moreover, the proposal suggested that the new degree program could be implemented with no significant increase in costs. No plan of program evaluation was presented, and the proposal had not been reviewed by any professionals external to the university. Only one of the relevant faculty members held an earned doctorate.

Though a discomforting act for her first week on the job, the president wisely and appropriately returned the proposal for further work, suggesting that the presence of a new facility was hardly sufficient justification for a new program. A leadership expectation of excellence was integral to this president's action.

A professor of sociology invited to be a member of a doctoral committee was presented with a draft of the student's dissertation six weeks before the student's intended graduation date in the spring, with the defense set in one week. Noting that a wide range of conclusions were based on a simple tabulation of means, offered without benefit of any standard for evaluation—statistical, expert opinion, or other—the committee member suggested to the student that perhaps the doctoral defense had been scheduled prematurely. Additional analysis might be needed to support the conclusions presented. This advice provoked a response from the committee chair that can only be described as ungracious. Maybe wiser than his mentor, however, the student accurately sensed the need for additional analytical rigor, though his graduation date was postponed by a term. The additional analysis produced from the same data conclusions that were completely opposite from the initial analysis and evaluation. Even the chair's resistance softened in the face of this result, but only because his committee colleague had met the test: the expectation of excellence.

A newly minted assistant professor of political science gave his first exam. While wandering the back of the room, he spotted one of his students glancing at his shirt sleeve with some frequency, a suspicious action considering that this was the end of the spring and short-sleeve shirts were more compatible with the relatively hot and humid weather. A member of the university's baseball team, the student was also not known for his spiffy dressing habits. Cotton-mesh casual shirts, walking shorts, and sandals were more often seen than his attire for today's test day—white shirt, blue blazer, regimental tie, gray slacks, and tassel loafers. Alarm bells began to ring in the belfry of our new assistant professor, and he wracked his brain for memory of some training or experience that might guide his actions.

Should he call the student out and accuse him of cheating? An option of questionable merit. Might he ask to inspect what appeared to be a helpful shirt cuff? Again, a tactic of uncertain but potentially dangerous valence. Might he depend on the observations and witness of students around the offending scholar as a means of fingering the cheater? Would the honor code work? Might he ignore the incident and concentrate instead on the journal article needing his attention so that he could traverse a more certain and speedy path to tenure and associate professor? A safe and easy option.

He decided instead on a test of performance and invited the student over to his office for coffee and conversation after the passage of a couple of days, a salutary and friendly professorial gesture. "This analysis on first amendment rights and hate speech codes was interesting," the assistant professor opened. "You didn't really get into the 'fighting words' test suggested by the 1942 Supreme Court ruling on *Chaplinsky* v. *New Hampshire*. Do you see that ruling supporting your analysis?" In a moment, our young assistant professor will discover whether his baccalaureate scholar can do more than catch and throw baseballs—also a performance occupation. Indeed, it may be discovered whether this student is willing to honor in the classroom the same test he must live by on the baseball field, that of performance. And if he is thoughtful, our young professor will make contributions to both improvement and a standard of excellence in this exchange. If the student has cheated, what actions are suggested? Will our professor flunk the student on this examination or in the course? Or might he, in the spirit of improvement and performance, allow the student to field this play again?

The college president, the sociology professor, the political science professor, each of these will make a contribution not only to the idea of excellence but to an accompanying principle previously mentioned. In *The Spirit of Community*, Etzioni suggests that "all educational institutions, from kindergarten to universities, recognize and take seriously the grave responsibility to provide moral education" (1993, p. 258). Leadership is, I say again, a moral art form.

As a parenthetical note, I emphasize again that leadership is not a responsibility invested only in those holding formal administrative appointments, but a responsibility of all those holding climates of learning in trust—a responsibility of presidents and professors. Writing in *Stewardship*, Peter Block suggests that we need to put "leadership in the background where it belongs" and concentrate on stewardship, which "begins with the willingness to be accountable for some larger body than ourselves . . . when we choose service over self interest" (1993, p. 6). Yet that our best and most effective leaders are also servants and stewards is consistently reflected in the illustrations Block uses in his book. For example, Block cites the example of a chemical company executive who took over a struggling and nonprofitable organization and took steps to flatten the structure, create a participative culture, fully inform people, eliminate trappings of prestige, and define quality in customer-response terms; from my perspective, this case reveals not leadership in the background but leadership as servant and steward.

Since I earlier used a sports analogy in our conversation on the nature and nurture of excellence, what might we say about the excellence of the baseball team to which our young political science major will perhaps return? We can examine the won-loss record, and we can discern whether the team places in the conference tournament and travels to the collegiate world series in Omaha. The challenges of talent identification and development will certainly loom large in the record of the team. Great coaches, however, have always been more than collectors of talent. How they transform those skills into a team is as much a testimony to their competence as the identification of talent. Thus, leaders carry responsibility for expectations of excellence for the individuals who compose the "team" and also for the team itself. Let us turn to matters of organizational excellence.

The Nature and Nurture of Organizational Excellence

At least four streams of activity may be discerned in contemporary approaches to collegiate quality assurance:

- Traditional peer review evaluations
- Assessment and outcome movement
- Total quality management
- Accountability reporting

I would like to briefly explore each of these, add a fifth one to the list, and then propose a set of design principles that might assist in both strengthening and integrating our approaches to the achievement of quality at the organizational level.

Traditional Peer Review Evaluations

What indicators will we accept as evidence of quality? Writing in *Managing Quality* (1988), David Garvin recommends that such factors as fitness for use, reliability, conformance to specification, esthetics, durability, and so forth be employed in assessing the quality of industrial products. American higher education has fashioned several forms of evidence for excellence, including

- Accreditation—The test of mission and goal achievement
- Rankings and ratings—The test of reputation
- Program reviews—The test of peer evaluation
- Follow-up studies—The test of client satisfaction

Each of these has strengths and liabilities. Robert Saunders and I have explored these in greater detail in *The Evidence for Quality* (1992). Here I briefly note that the oldest and best-known seal of collegiate quality, accreditation, is built on the premise and the promise of mission integrity and performance improvement. Under frequent assault in contemporary literature for a range of imperfections, accreditation is described as an episodic exercise in professional back scratching built on minimalist standards, whose processes and activities are often hidden from public view. Ranking and rating studies, including the well-known *U.S. News & World Report* ratings of America's best colleges, keep the conversation on quality alive but are indicted for offering little help toward the goal of improved quality; the ratings have been referred to as quantified gossip. Student and alumni satisfaction indexes are a legitimate and essential evidence of quality; however, these may be inversely related to excellence in educational settings, a point to which we will return in a moment. While academic program reviews occupy a respected position, especially in the research university, they are often viewed by faculty as empty and futile exercises, busywork to occupy some assistant or associate administrator and to burden faculty.

The Assessment and Outcome Movement

Can we trust the anecdotal assertion conveyed in the American Management Association title *I'll Know Quality When I See It?* (Guaspari, 1985). Perhaps under some conditions. But we can do better than that. We can assemble concrete and specific evidence on quality. We can, and should, know as much about our students on exit as we do on entry—about changes in and the level of their knowledge, skill, and attitudes. The assessment movement in this country, a development primarily of the last ten to twenty years, centers on the acquisition of multiple indicators in the evaluation of both student and program performance.

In *Excellence,* Gardner notes that "the important thing to be borne in mind is that every known measure of aptitudes and achievements has some failings. Only by drawing upon a considerable variety of evidence can we be certain that our judgement is well-rounded and fair to the young person" (1984, p. 51). The nature of both personal and organizational performance is too complex to be captured in a single data point. Consider the leadership and educational posture of an accounting department chair

- Who knows that her students have the highest pass rate on the certified public accountant examination of any institution in her state
- Who has a rating of high satisfaction from graduates over recent years
- Whose files are filled with mostly complimentary letters from employers of her graduates
- Whose students regularly perform well on a campuswide assessment of communication and critical-thinking skills
- Whose department was praised and commended by a recent program review panel of accounting faculty members from peer institutions

This department chair has a cluster of assessment evidence, of performance intelligence, useful in making both decisions and educational improvements. As physicians do not have a health meter in their offices but evaluate our health by examining a body of medical information, so we need a range of performance assessments and evidence to make quality judgments about students, programs, and institutions.

The annual forums on assessment sponsored by the American Association for Higher Education and the increased presence of directors of planning and assessment on campuses attest to the emerging interest in the role of evaluation on American college and university campuses. Perhaps the most critical question remaining is whether assessment activities have been effectively linked to teaching and learning, to the improvement of what happens in our class-rooms, laboratories, and studios. The 1993 Jossey-Bass publication *Making a Difference* (Banta and Associates, 1993) offers diverse institutional illustrations that support the constructive impact of the movement. Institutions such as Alverno College and Northeast Missouri State University furnish affirming models of how assessment can become an intimate and effective instrument of learning. There are too many institutions, however, still going through the motions of collecting assessment data on students and programs but failing to link that information to decisions.

Total Quality Management (TQM)

The term *total quality management* (TQM), also referred to as strategic quality management, has emerged from the work of writers that include W. Edwards Deming, W. A. Shewart, Philip Crosby, Joseph Juran, Kaoru Ishikana, and David Garvin. An illuminating and integrating work, one offering a favorable treatment of TQM as applied to higher education, is Daniel Seymour's *On Q: Causing Quality in Higher Education* (1992). Seymour is convinced that "accrediting agencies, program reviews, standing committees, control-minded governing boards, and the occasional well-intentioned task force" will not be the instruments for creating quality in higher education (1992, p. x). He proposes TQM as an answer to his question "Is there a better way to manage higher education?"

Seymour's advocacy of TQM warrants thoughtful review. Seymour suggests that current and conventional quality instruments, such as program reviews and accreditation, make little significant contribution to college quality. He sees these instruments as occasional devices that convey the appearance of quality and that establish a "good enough" mindset. Those who have been on both the giving and receiving end of program and accreditation reviews will know the liabilities of these and other "evidence" of quality previously cited in this chapter. Both these instruments are built, however, on the premise and promise of improvement, an idea central to TQM and one of the governing ideals of quality emphasized in this chapter.

Is it necessary to deprecate the contributions of quality assur-

ance instruments already in place in order to appreciate what TQM
has to offer? I think not. Space constraints do not permit scrutiny
of all the principles cited for TQM. Having accented the principle
of continuous improvement, we elect to examine two additional
ideas from TQM. With respect to the driving principle of TQM,
that of customer-client satisfaction, few would argue that we listen
enough to our students and other clients. Nevertheless, there are
critical differences between corporate and collegiate settings in the
application of this principle. Faculty members who have found
their desire to care for students in tension with caring for standards
know the limitation of this quality test for colleges and universities.
Students do indeed, as Seymour suggests, vote with their feet. It is
sad when they occasionally vote for shoddy and shallow options;
when they do, the ideal of quality should not be exchanged for the
notion of satisfaction.

Advocates of TQM often cite the idea that everyone has a
customer. Some of those are internal; others are external. Thus,
TQM training will usually involve the identification of "customers" by those who hold staff and support functions, such as registrar
and finance officers. In an article appearing in the June 1993 issue
of *Management Review,* Harari criticizes this position: "Like a
vampire who refuses to die, the "internal customer" continues to
rear its ugly head. I still get letters and documents from individuals
who argue that the goal of customer satisfaction applies to both
internal and external customers, and that the road to delighted external customers is paved with the satisfaction of internal ones. I
admit the theory sounds rosy, but like some other theories in management, this one has little basis in reality and in practice may be
downright dangerous" (1993, p. 30).

And in *Stewardship,* Peter Block shows how bureaucracies
can bulge in serving those internal customers. One company re-
duced its corporate headquarters staff, all busy serving internal customers, from four thousand to four hundred. Block comments,
"Don't call them a customer if they have no choice. . . . Calling
people you can demand a response from a 'customer' is manipula-
tion . . . using the language of consideration to soften the coercion
in the relationship" (1993, p. 125).

Now a word on problem solving. Many campuses are trying

TQM. Some faculty and administrative officers see TQM as appropriate for improvements in the admissions office, the business
office, the facilities maintenance office, the campus security office,
or other administrative settings; but others note, as does Seymour,
that these are not the only settings where "we degrade, we hassle,
and we ignore" (p. 115). Will we be as quick to see opportunities
for listening to our clients, for continuously improving, for problem solving in the academic heart of colleges and universities? Our
students can be placed in harm's way by low and empty expectations, by assessment exercises having little or no decision utility, by
a vision of quality depending more on faculty publication counts
than teaching and caring for our students. This is an issue that
collegiate leaders can legitimately explore.

    Whether the initial euphoria and the subsequent quiet pas-
sage of some previously heralded management concepts will eventually also describe the fate of TQM in colleges and universities
remains to be seen. An argument can be made that many of the
philosophical principles of TQM have been at work in academia for
some time. The quest for quality will always remain an unfinished
journey, and there is no reason to neglect any conceptual tool that
will aid us in that quest. As with any tool, the effectiveness of its
application turns on the artistry of the user in ensuring that it fits
the time, task, and place.

    As an interesting aside, consensus has not been achieved on
the application of TQM in corporate sector organizations. In an
article appearing in the January 1993 issue of *Management Review*
entitled "Ten Reasons Why TQM Doesn't Work," Oren Harari
comments, "TQM is only one of many possible means to obtain
quality. In other words, quality is sacred; TQM is not. There's
another difference: as we shall see, quality is about unbending focus, passion, iron discipline and a way of life for all hands. TQM
is about statistics, jargon, committees and quality departments"
(p. 33).

    This critique of TQM in the corporate sector strikes me as
another instance where we are unhappily inclined to throw out the
baby with the bath water. Yet it also reminds us of an equally
unfortunate tendency, prevalent in both the corporate and collegiate worlds: seize the latest management fad and associated acro-

nym as the cure for all ills. My previous comments suggest that there are useful lessons to be gleaned from TQM philosophy and others if approached with a great deal of care.

One other postscript to Harari's notes I would offer. While the metaphor of corporate and collegiate leaders orchestrating organizational voices and serving as musical maestros can be a confining one, I would like for the moment to retain the image, for I think it contains a useful truth.

It is possible for an individual musician or an ensemble of any size, including a full orchestra, to play correctly: that is, with zero defects (as the statistical process control folks would say, "in control and capable"). But this is not musical quality. In the orchestra hall, customers are patrons. And patrons know that correct music is not necessarily quality music. If the music lacks passion and fire, inventiveness and imagination, "correctness" will not transform a dull and uninspired performance into a good one. In the orchestra hall of the university, will our students not also be able to discern when we are correct and when we care?!

Accountability Reporting

It is clear that state governments are increasingly concerned with the question of excellence. A study published by the Southern Regional Education Board (SREB) in 1993, for example, indicates that public colleges and universities in all but two of the fifteen states in SREB region now have either a legislative or other requirement for an annual comprehensive accountability report (Bogue, Folger, Creech, 1993). The shift in state policy interests among the states is described in the SREB report as follows:

> In the 1960s and 1970s, state higher education policy centered on the planned expansion of higher education and the promotion of equity in access. In the 1980s, the focus shifted to improving quality. . . . In the 1990s, state policy interests moved toward
>
> • The assessment of educational performance and outcomes

- The development of new higher education accountability measures
- The improvement of management and educational productivity
- The refocus and revision of campus missions and the reallocation of resources from lower to higher priority programs [p. 3]

The SREB report goes on to indicate that an evaluation of these state accountability policies has yet to occur, and the following questions are posed:

- Have state policies, for example, produced constructive and substantive changes at the campus level, or have campus responses been largely cosmetic and adaptive?
- Has the implementation of state accountability policies led to increased awareness of, confidence in, and support of higher education?
- Are political and educational leaders using the extensive accountability reporting?
- Do states have policies that support improvement in both favorable and unfavorable economic times, and do these policies survive changes in leadership at the executive level? (p. 12).

It is also clear that governing boards for both public and private institutions are becoming more interested in the expectation of excellence. Among six major recommendations of the report *Trustees and Troubled Times in Higher Education* (1992) published by the Association of Governing Boards of Universities and Colleges is this one: "How can this institution set new standards of quality?" (pp. 22-23). The report chides the higher education community for emphasizing only one model of excellence, driven by the prestige of research: "Quality is measured more by the kinds of students excluded and turned down than by the kinds of students included and turned out. . . . Quality, in short, has become something to stoke academic egos instead of students 'dreams' " (p. 22).

The Ethical Dimension of Quality

In *The Evidence for Quality,* Robert Saunders and I recommend an ethical test in our definition of quality: "Quality is conformance to mission specification and goal achievement—within publicly accepted standards of accountability and integrity" (1992, p. 20). Our reason for including an ethical test was as follows: "Can we claim, in either a corporate or collegiate setting, to produce quality while we are busy stealing from ourselves, our government, and our customers and clients? We think not" (p. 21). Let me take this argument a step further via a quick illustration.

Years ago, I remember being invited to the office of the graduate dean at Memphis State University, Dr. John Richardson. Dr. Richardson was a splendid educator who had made a lifelong investment in Tennessee education at every level; he was known far and wide as a man of integrity, competence, high standards, and personal caring. He was the man most directly responsible for my being in higher education. Dr. Richardson was one of the more important mentors in my life, a professional and personal model to whom I tender affection and respect.

On this particular day, I found Dean Richardson on the phone, apparently with one of our state senators. I gathered from listening to one side of the conversation that the senator wanted a student admitted to graduate school, someone who did not meet the regular admission standards. After trying a persuasive approach with Dean Richardson, the senator seemed to switch to a more threatening tactic. My inference concerning the switch in the senator's tactics came from both watching Dean Richardson's visage and listening to his response. His bulldog-like jowls began to shake, and he said, "Son, are you threatening me? Because if you are, I will come up there to Big Sandy and campaign against you when you come up for reelection next year. And, son, I will defeat you." And he would have. Dean Richardson carried a wagonload of respect all over the state (and especially in West Tennessee).

Was this a quality issue? I think that it was. But it had nothing to do with the traditional approaches of accreditation and the concept of peer review, nothing to with assessment and multiple evidences, nothing to do with TQM and customer satisfaction, and nothing to do with accountability reporting. It was about character! Now this lesson in collegiate leadership does not appear on my college transcript, but it may have been a more powerful lesson than the theories represented in the graduate courses that do appear there.

The expectation for excellence has both technical and ethical dimensions! And the effective collegiate leader will tend to both.

Excellence by Design

What questions can college leaders use to evaluate quality assurance policies and programs on the campus or campuses for which they are responsible? Here are themes and questions to help examine campus commitment to excellence and quality assurance, a summary look at the governing ideals we have been exploring.

Distinction in Mission

Does the campus have a distinctive mission statement? Questions of ends encourage questions of beginnings. Inquiries concerning performance will eventually lead to those of purpose. The architecture of the campus mission furnishes an essential foundation for an effective quality assurance effort. Does the campus have a crisp statement of mission and values that clearly and forcefully reveals what it stands for? If the content of the mission statement is so vague and indistinctive that it could describe a hundred other campuses, we may certainly have the origins of a quality problem.

Our assumptions about excellence and quality shape the reality in which we seek to nurture quality. For example, the belief that quality is in limited supply contradicts the idea that it is attainable and essential to each and every campus. It argues against the idea that quality will always be related to mission and that this, no matter how comprehensive, will always be limited. That a campus or campus system will have units or programs that differ in mission is understandable. The existence of "second class" units and programs is more difficult to defend. The search for varieties of excellence is a key and critical principle in the definition, the assessment, and the nurture of quality.

From Stanford University in the West to Samford University
in the East, from the University of Michigan in the North to the
University of Montevallo in the South, from Massachusetts Institute
of Technology in the Northeast to Maricopa Community College
in the Southwest, from Centenary College to Central Piedmont
Community College, from the Air Force Academy to Antioch—
anyone who takes in the grand sweep of American higher education
will immediately and intuitively sense the folly of our conventional
pyramidal models of collegiate excellence and will come to respect
the governing ideal of varieties of excellence in both individual and
institutional performance. Other ideas related to institutional excellence (the relationship between cost and excellence, for example),
are put to the test by Pascarella and Terrenzini in their major work
How College Affects Students (1990) and in a more condensed journal version (1992).

Evidence of Improvement

Can the campus offer evidence of improvements that have been
made to program and policy as a result of assessment and quality
inquiries? The improvement question is one that should be posed
and answered for every organized unit on campus. A campus or
program unit that cannot offer a reasonably prompt and substantive
answer to that question deserves skepticism about the strength and
substance of its quality assurance efforts. Any assessment or quality
assurance endeavor that does not have decision utility is an empty
exercise.

Linkage to Teaching and Learning

How have quality inquiries been used to improve teaching and
learning, to enhance the growth and development of students, the
faculty, and the staff? Are quality assurance and assessment activities "faculty friendly"? We will not have to search our memories
very deeply to remember who the primary architects of quality are.
They are the professors who elevated our vision and pushed us to
realize our potential. Assessment and quality assurance exercises
unconnected to teaching and learning are also empty.

External Standards

In the early history of American higher education, one of the principal board member roles was to examine the proposed graduates. Thus, to the judgments and standards of the faculty was added the external standard of the board. The employment of external standards continues to be found in externally referenced assessment efforts and the use of external teams in accreditation and program reviews. There is a philosophical tension inherent in this governing ideal. Some contemporary philosophies of quality (total quality management, for example) justifiably insist that those responsible for the product are also responsible for quality. Is it a misplacement of trust to insert a third party or external standard into the quality assurance process? I think not. An essential feature of the academy is testing ideas against the larger community of scholars. The results of our work must come into the public forum at some time.

Multiple Evidences

An effective quality assurance program will involve the acquisition of multiple indicators of both student and program performance. Does the campus have a variety of high-quality evidence—conventional tests, program reviews, accreditation, licensure results, client satisfaction and follow-up studies, student portfolios, and perhaps other innovative and imaginative intelligence on student and program performance? Alexander Astin (1985) suggests that what a campus elects to evaluate and how to do so furnish a philosophical window into what it values. What do our approaches to assessment tell us about ourselves?

Strategic and Systemic Perspective

Does the campus have a strategic and unifying vision of quality? This vision will be built on the idea that there is no policy, behavior, or practice that does not influence quality. Moreover, there will be a coherent and logical system of interactions among the various institutional approaches to quality assurance. The philosophy and components of the quality assurance system will reflect the awareness and allegiance of the faculty and staff.

There are other dimensions of this ideal of systemic perspective that warrant our attention. Well-intentioned and competent professionals may not deliver quality if they are part of bad systems. Recall the illustration cited in Chapter Two on the enrollment system at City College. Are good and able people serving a bad registration or academic policy system, for example? In the spirit of the design role earlier cited for leadership, then, collegiate leaders interested in achieving quality will ensure that competent individuals are appointed to examine and evaluate the performance of systems on campus. With due apology to the custodians of simple English, university leaders will also be alert to the examination of what some call suprasystems. For instance, students will experience their introduction to a college or university through a suprasystem of enrollment services that may include admissions, financial aid, records and registration, and finance and accounting systems. The quality of enrollment services may depend upon effective interactions between and among these areas. And it may call for leaders whose role is to manage suprasystem functions.

A campus whose quality assurance efforts salute these governing ideals will have experienced their renewal power. Such a campus will have rediscovered purpose and priority, promoted the development of its faculty and staff via continued learning, and strengthened community. There can be no quality in an educational enterprise without caring, and there can be no caring without community.

Heart First: A Vision of Individual and Organizational Excellence

College leaders can ascertain whether campuses under their care can offer a range of evidence of excellence; whether these campuses can demonstrate policy, program, and personnel improvements that have been made as a result of quality inquiry; and whether educational and management decisions are being informed by information on quality. These are conceptual or "head first" concerns, and they are among the important governing ideals of excellence and quality cited in this chapter.

But the principal guarantors of excellence and quality are "heart first" actions of caring and daring:

> The promise of quality resides, then, in the plain of our passions. Do we care enough for truth, do we care enough for service, and do we care enough for human growth and dignity that our vision of quality permeates the entire campus and touches the mind and heart of every person who serves there? Will that vision yield standards and encouragement that call our students and our colleagues from the poverty of the commonplace, that salute the promise of each one on the campus (whether student or staff), and that launch each person to the far reaches of his or her potential? Will that vision reveal a happy curiosity and active compassion? Will that vision marry a respect for diversity of mission and talent with a scorn for shoddy work, whether individual or institutional? And will that vision respond not to the intellectual call to advance the truth but to the ethical call of justice, dignity, integrity, and nobility? The promise can only be realized in a community of caring, which ought to be an accurate descriptor of a quality college or university [Bogue and Saunders, 1992, p. 280].

In *Sand and Foam,* Kahlil Gibran writes, "Your heart and my mind will never agree until your mind ceases to live in numbers and my heart in the mist" (1973, p. 30). Not all that is real or meaningful or beautiful in colleges, universities, and other learning organizations, will yield to quantification. There are, however, design principles that enable collegiate leaders to encourage personal and organizational excellence and to engage questions of student and program performance more effectively. The discovery and decision promise of the design principles presented in this chapter will unfold only in the hands of those collegiate leaders who have the expectation of excellence.

8

The Servant Exemplar

I cannot think of any contemporary books that more effectively represent the poles of leadership values and effectiveness than two already cited in these chapters: James Stewart's *Den of Thieves* (1991) and Colby and Damon's *Some Do Care* (1992). The first of these details the insider-trading scandal that rocked Wall Street and the duplicity of four brokers (Michael Milken, Ivan Boesky, Martin Siegel, and Dennis Levine) whose integrity regrettably did not match their financial brilliance. In the second book are the extraordinary stories of five very different American leaders and moral exemplars: Suzie Valdez, Virginia Durr, Jack Coleman, Charleszetta Waddles, and Cabell Brand. The deeds and lives of the moral exemplars in *Some Do Care* contrast sharply with the greed and duplicity of the financial leaders profiled in *Den of Thieves*.

These two books are also chronicles of leadership effectiveness, of the ways men and women have chosen to invest their lives, and of the means leaders use to measure their success. "What makes a life significant?" is a question posed early in Joseph Epstein's *Ambition:* "There is the standard of the cash box. There is the standard of good works. There is the standard of public opinion. There is the standard of harmlessness, of doing little to make life poorer for one's fellows. There is the standard of altering history, of changing the life of one's time. There is the standard of being, in some ineffable way, a force" (1980, p. 40).

When leaders begin their responsibilities, an important first question involves role: what they are supposed to do. Thus, theories of role are important in shaping the subsequent behaviors of collegiate leaders. From the very first day of our leadership responsibilities, however, a second kind of theory will be active in guiding our behavior—a theory of effectiveness. How will success be judged? In the spirit of Epstein's question, by what criteria and standards will those holding leadership responsibility measure the significance of their lives, the effectiveness of their leadership investment? This is a question of majestic import for leaders in both corporate and collegiate settings and one for engagement in this closing chapter.

The Ideal of Service

To be an American, in the minds of many, has meant that we always stand for something, that there are enduring ideals that give us common cause in the midst of our diversity. In my mind, it is impossible to consider the question of leadership effectiveness without embracing in that question the moral posture of the leader. "What do we stand for?" is no idle inquiry in my vision of leadership effectiveness. Thus, in this volume, I have attempted to explore those ideals that reveal leadership as a moral art form, those values that promote the probability of effective performance for the collegiate leader—no matter where or in what position he or she may serve. To the ideals of effective leadership examined in previous chapters, I add here the ideal of service.

The leader who neglects or abandons the servant ideal will sooner or later fall victim to arrogance, and the departure of her or his nobility will manifest itself in destructive behavior. In previous chapters, I have provided several illustrations of collegiate leaders neglecting or abandoning the service ideal. One such departure from the standard of service is one too many! Academic leaders who invest their early attention in worrying about the size of the office, the appearance of the calling card, the location of a reserved parking place, and a box seat at the stadium telegraph a potential neglect of the servant motive. Other more damaging behavioral consequences may be predicted from these early signs of a leader more interested in serving self than others.

Readers interested in a psychological interpretation of hubris in the life of our leaders will find Kets de Vries's book *Leaders, Fools, and Imposters* (1993) an interesting excursion. He comments, "Hubris is a recurring theme in leadership, for the obvious reason that excessive pride and arrogance often accompany power" (p. 93). Kets de Vries suggests that leaders were historically often led to see and guard against their arrogance by those who played the role of fools (hence the word *fools* in the title of his book). A review of the role of the fool in Shakespeare's *As You Like It* and *King Lear* shows us how "with the use of humor, fools can do the otherwise unthinkable, trespassing on forbidden territory and satirizing both leaders and followers" (Kets de Vries, 1993, p. 99).

Whether we are ready for a position description of fool in our college personnel rosters and records is a matter open to question. Might such a position be a relatively high-salaried one, close to that of an associate dean or associate vice president? Well, perhaps not. We do not need to add administrative positions, and there are simpler and less expensive ways to guard against hubris. Independent and technically competent men and women, colleagues who respect the leadership design ideals of candor and courage and who have a lively sense of humor (and perhaps mischievous spirits), are to be preferred over sycophants within the immediate circle of those who advise leaders and hold them accountable. My prescription for guarding against the seductive call of power and arrogance includes also a respect for the design ideal of service.

What are the qualities that mark the servant leader? A classic reference on this subject certainly has to be Robert Greenleaf's 1977 book by that same title. Early in that book, Greenleaf offers this reflection: "A new moral principle is emerging which holds that the only authority deserving one's allegiance is that which is freely and knowingly granted by the led to the leader in response to, and in proportion to, the clearly evident servant stature of the leader. Those who choose to follow this principle will not casually accept the authority of existing institutions. Rather, they will freely respond only to individuals who are chosen as leaders because they are proven and trusted as servants" (1977, p. 10).

Though recognized as perhaps the foremost contemporary advocate of servant leadership, Greenleaf is not the first to adopt this perspective, as anyone who has encountered this biblical verse will recognize: "And whosoever will be chief among you, let him be your servant" (Matthew 20:27). Or these lines from Stephen Mitchell's translation of Lao-Tzu's *Tao Te Ching:* "If you want to govern the people, you must place yourself below them. If you want to lead the people, you must learn how to follow them" (1988, p. 56). Aaron Copeland's bright and brassy musical salute "Fanfare for the Common Man" makes good theme music for the servant leader.

Here at the University of Tennessee are many who might be described as servant leaders. One among them is Dr. John Prados, professor of chemical engineering, department chair, system vice president, and interim chancellor of several campuses in the system. I have known John for twenty of the more than thirty years he has served the University of Tennessee at Knoxville and the University of Tennessee system. He is a leader who has demonstrated his competence and caring in both faculty and executive roles. He is a man devoted to family.

In addition to his work for the university, John has served the profession of engineering and the interests of American higher education in a variety of regional, national, and international roles and responsibilities. He is a professional whose every behavior shows caring and integrity. He is a man of honor, a servant exemplar, a collegiate leader who will never have to be concerned about a test of significance or effectiveness for his life or his leadership.

Since I began by emphasizing the critical import of every leader's having a theory of effectiveness, one that has been opened to examination, let me turn more directly now to the work of defining and discerning leadership effectiveness. What we find will not be unfriendly to the concept and criteria of servant leadership.

The Definition of Leader Effectiveness

When one asks how the effectiveness of leaders should be judged, a frequent response is "How are you defining effectiveness?" The definition question will eventually occupy the attention of every leader, no matter what organization or cause he or she may serve and no matter at what level.

As I worked on this chapter, I enjoyed reading Martin Gilbert's summary biography of Winston Churchill (1991). The defeat of the Conservative party in the summer of 1945 and Churchill's consequent loss of the prime minister's position immediately following his extraordinary and inspiring leadership of Britain during World War II is a surprising moment of history, and certainly one that must have left Churchill reflecting on the issue of leadership effectiveness.

As a matter of contrasting interest, we might take note of a new biography of Churchill by John Charmley. Mr. Charmley undertakes to debunk what he describes as the Churchill myth: that Churchill was a great leader, that Hitler was a singular form of evil, and that the British empire was destined to collapse. The book has been reviewed as both a major contribution and a collection of hogwash. My point here is to emphasize that evaluating the effectiveness of leaders is an exercise always subject to controversy. This verity, however, only accents the need for each leader to construct a personal philosophy of effectiveness.

In addition to this remarkable story of history and biography, other events have inspired me to think about leadership effectiveness in more serious fashion. One of these was my resignation as chancellor of LSU in Shreveport after serving in that position for ten and a half years. What philosophy of effectiveness did I take to the position in the summer of 1980, and what evidence of leadership effectiveness did I count important as I departed the position in December of 1990? To these questions, I will return in a moment.

I was fortunate enough to experience a dignified exit from the chancellor's position and a renewing call to teaching. If I am an effective teacher, I will assist and encourage my students to decide what *they* stand for—to ensure that there are concepts in their heads, caring in their hands, and conviction in their hearts. In a *National Forum* article, Martha Tack warns against the dangers possible here: "We should not allow those who have served as 'headmen' to continue perpetuating and 'birthing' leaders like themselves" (1991, p. 30). I have no interest in the construction of clones.

I do have an interest in encouraging my students to fashion their own philosophy of role, style, and effectiveness.

Effectiveness: A Look at the Literature

Among the conceptual offerings on our theme are first those focusing on the performance measurements of leadership effectiveness. For example, in his classic *The Functions of the Executive,* Chester Barnard observes that the executive should be judged by the accomplishment of recognized objectives (1938). In a 1978 commentary, Hollander suggests that the effectiveness of the leader should be assessed by the relationship between organizational performance and potential. And in *Leadership: The Inner Side of Greatness,* Koestenbaum notes, "Effectiveness means that you are obligated to achieve results with your organization" (1991, p. 201). By contrast, John Gardner offers a conditioning view that "consequences are not a reliable measure of leadership"; he points to the qualifying influences of time and climate (1990, p. 8). In difficult financial or political environments, college leaders who would ordinarily welcome the "results" test of effectiveness might also welcome Gardner's caveat.

Among those works that dwell on the characteristics of effective leaders is Peter Drucker's widely read and oft-cited *The Effective Executive.* Drucker remarks that the effective executive knows how his or her time is spent, focuses on results, builds on strengths, concentrates on a few goals, and makes effective decisions (1966, pp. 23–24). Distilling the best thought from a number of writers, scholars, and practitioners on management and leadership theory, Hitt offers a leadership assessment inventory that measures leadership performance in several areas. Among the personal attributes used to describe the effective leader are these: she or he is self-confident, self-motivated, and self-directing; is a person of purpose and commitment; is action oriented; is guided by a clear set of values; is willing to "stand up and be counted"; is decisive; is a person of integrity; and is a continual learner (1988, pp. 219–230).

A third stream of research centers on leadership styles and effectiveness. Here one finds the widely cited works of such writers as Blake and Mouton (1964), Fiedler (1967), Reddin (1970), and

Hersey (1984). Bolman and Deal (1991) offer an insightful and eval-
uative analysis of these style theories and suggest that effective
leaders view organizations through multiple frames—structural,
human resource, political, and symbolic (goals, people, power, and
symbols). In the more effective manifestation of these four frames,
leaders are (respectively) social architects, servants, advocates, and
prophets-poets. In their least effective manifestation, leaders are ty-
rants, wimps, con artists, and fanatics. While political and symbolic
frames seem particularly important in effective leadership and organizations, sensitivity to and use of all four frames are essential
(Bolman and Deal, 1991).

   In one of the more thoughtful and instructive books on leadership in collegiate settings, Donald Walker (1979) writes in *The
Effective Administrator* that ineffective collegiate leaders are occupied with status and position, regard critics as troublemakers, see
their role as one of having to make unpopular decisions, and are
occupied with opposing laziness and inertia. By contrast, effective
leaders wear the symbols of privilege and office lightly, view their
role as one of reconciling dissent, do not make enemies out of dis-
senters, see the university in a healthy political sense, are confident
and assured, and assume that the university as an organization is
healthy rather than pathological.

   Empirical approaches to the identification of effective collegiate leadership include the 1986 book *Searching for Academic Excellence*; Gilley, Fulmer, and Reithlingshoefer paint a composite
picture of presidents providing leadership to campuses on the move.
The authors identify certain characteristics in the presidents of excellent institutions. These individuals like face-to-face contact with
people deep in the organization and are not inclined to be inhibited
by the confines of organizational charts. They create a visible presence on the campus and model what Peters and Waterman (1982)
describe in their earlier book, *In Search of Excellence,* as "management by walking about." These presidents are further described as
"conservative gamblers," willing to work out front but taking every
step to minimize risk. They create a safety zone of goodwill and trust
that will allow them to behave occasionally in a unilateral and
authoritarian manner. Finally, the effective presidents were de-

scribed by their faculties and staffs as men and women with a personal, caring, and compassionate touch (1986).

Echoing some of these findings, Fisher and Tack (1988) assert that effective college presidents are extremely self-confident and positive, are deeply committed to the mission of their campuses, show confidence in colleagues, are risk takers but not reckless, are strategists and concerned with broad visions, are not bound by current structures, and have the willingness to move against mainstream currents. Their findings are based on a national study of effective and ineffective presidents.

For college presidents and other collegiate leaders, there will be many serving on the jury of leadership effectiveness—faculty members, students, administrative colleagues, alumni, board members, civic and political officials. As I noted in an earlier chapter, responding to the performance expectations of so many constituencies is a contextual condition of leadership that may be unique to collegiate life. At whatever level of their engagement, most collegiate leaders will eventually realize that they can get in trouble at least three different ways: technical-conceptual liabilities (relieved from duty because of ignorance), ethical-moral liabilities (relieved from duty because of irresponsibility), and cultural-environmental liabilities (relieved from duty because of insensitivity). We can learn from reading and reflection, and we can learn from action and experience. What reflections on effectiveness have I gleaned from my own leadership journey?

Effectiveness: A Personal Reflection

In my University of Tennessee leadership seminar, we explore the idea that there is no unfiltered reality: the leader's values and philosophical dispositions create a social reality. Theory becomes prophecy. The aspiration of the seminar experience is to have the students make their philosophy accessible to their own consciousness—open to examination and affirmation, to challenge and change. My students are willing to take this journey but want to know if I will do the same. They know that I served in administrative roles for twenty-six years, ten of those in an executive role. How did I judge my own performance? How did I assess how good a job

I had done? Here are the first-formed frames of the answers to my students' questions.

The Condition of Longevity/Survival

Would I base the answer to the question of effectiveness on the raw datum of survival, the fact that I was in office for ten and a half years? In part, yes—caveats on the merit of longevity notwithstanding. Yet this time-in-service indicator of effectiveness is anchored in the conviction that effective leadership must be built on long-term investments and commitment. Among the "seven deadly diseases" of contemporary American management identified by W. Edwards Deming are those of lack of constancy of purpose and the mobility of top management (Walton, 1986). It takes time to make a difference. I have emphasized in an earlier chapter the importance of persistence. Perhaps, then, time inservice can be a legitimate condition of effectiveness.

Over a year after I left office as chancellor at LSU Shreveport, Dean Larry Clark of the College of Business there called to share the good news that the college had finally received accreditation by the American Association of Collegiate Schools of Business. We had worked on that goal for each of the ten years I served as chancellor and labored with many disappointments as the recessionary economic conditions in Louisiana greased the steep slope we were trying to climb—producing leadership challenges in recruiting and retaining faculty. The character of Dean Clark and his faculty was reflected not in their dreams but in their determination. They stayed the course, affirming the idea previously presented that leadership is not necessarily something others do for or to us but something we do together in shared ventures of purpose, persistence, and pleasure. This linkage of persistence and longevity of service to goal achievement allows a nice segue to the next indicator of effectiveness.

The Condition of Mission and Goal Achievement

As many writers have noted, one can be an officeholder and not be a leader. Occupation without outcome is no mark of leadership. As I look back over my career at LSU Shreveport, it seems to me that there are definitive achievement entries on the books: several new academic and student service programs begun, new academic appeals and faculty appeals processes placed in action, a quality assurance policy and practice implemented, a summer orientation program for freshmen and a counseling center established, an intercollegiate athletic program approved and implemented, a new faculty governance system and senate implemented, three new buildings funded (including a $12 million new library in my final year of service).

It took, however, ten years to set the stage for the construction of that building and to acquire the multimillion dollar endowment and private collection of some 200,000 volumes that would go in that new library. We built the university's first foundation and moved private-dollar acquisitions from a base of virtually zero to an income of over $1 million per year; the funding included significant private support of a network of four public radio stations, also built during that period.

The Condition of Organizational Integrity

The integrity record of the university is an important indicator, of course. During my period of service, the university experienced not a single audit exception in the yearly legislative audits of the university's financial and administrative operations. No member of the university's faculty or staff was ever cited in any document, media story, or other report for any act of educational, financial, or management wrongdoing during that ten-and-a-half years. This was an ethical record that saluted the integrity of the faculty and staff of the university. As former president of Indiana University Herman Wells suggests in his book about his long-lived presidency (1980), I was also lucky.

The Condition of Faculty-Staff Diversity

To my mind, an increase in faculty and staff diversity is yet another benchmark of performance progress. When I accepted appointment as chancellor in 1980, the university had one black faculty member in a faculty of some 170, and there were no black administrators.

There was only one black member on the eighteen-member chancellor's community advisory board for a university serving a metropolitan area that was 40 percent minority. During a few years, we would recruit ten black faculty members, three black administrators, and seven black members on the advisory board. Two of my three vice chancellors were women; one of my five deans was a woman. The university made some progress, but the journey for dignity and equity was incomplete.

The Condition of Constituent Satisfaction

How about the indicator of client satisfaction, the standard of public opinion to which Epstein refers? In the final days of my appointment, I received formal resolutions of appreciation from the university faculty senate, the alumni board, the mayor of the city of Shreveport, and the LSU board (from which I received the designation chancellor emeritus). I carry in my private files personal and informal notes from individual members of the faculty and staff, and letters from friends in both civic and academic life. I also treasure an affectionate farewell from custodians in the administration building, affirming expressions from members of the secretarial staff, and pleasant dinner moments with friends who furnished counsel and inspiration in difficult moments. There were well-wishing phone calls from political friends in the city and state, with whom I had jousted over the years and with whom I shared the intimate knowledge that our critics and opponents are often friends in disguise. Finally, there was that personal visit from a member of the university faculty who had been among the most vocal in the "loyal opposition" over the years. He told me that he appreciated my creating a climate in which he could express his dissent without fear of threat or reprisal.

The Condition of Leadership Climate

My final year in office featured approval and implementation of a long-pursued intercollegiate athletic program, the long-sought new library, and a 12 percent salary increase for faculty. These pleasant events, however, followed more challenging years. No leader exists in a cultural, political, and economic vacuum. Thus, in my personal assessment of leadership effectiveness are memories of an eight-year economic recession in Shreveport and in Louisiana. During this time, we raised student fees seven times, the faculty went three years without a raise, and the university sustained seven mid-year budget cuts. In addition, the entire higher education system of the state labored under legal uncertainty occasioned by a still-unresolved federal court suit related to desegregation.

The governance structure of the state remained under siege during four of those years, as the governor sought to eliminate the three governing boards and the coordinating board and replace them with a single board. One gubernatorial budget offered the prospect of closing the university, and one state task force entertained the idea of merging LSU Shreveport and other institutions. The sustained financial recession in the metropolitan area of Shreveport made it more difficult to raise private money and kept all public and private sector executives under the common challenge of maintaining optimism and community in a climate not conducive to either.

While these structural, financial, and political conditions pushed my optimism to its raw edge on many a day, I do not remember that we used these conditions as reasons for neglecting our responsibilities to move the university forward. Given these complicating and constraining environmental factors, the program, policy, and facility achievements and the progress of the larger university testify even more forcibly to the ability and character of the university's faculty and staff.

The Condition of Colleague Growth and Development

Another indicator of leadership effectiveness important to me is reflected in the personal growth of the men and women with whom I served. The record of my mentor role is modest compared to that of many presidential friends, but it remains a source of private satisfaction. The growth of faculty and staff colleagues and the development of students are important indicators of leadership effectiveness. Leaders are teachers. Teachers are learners.

The Lessons of Our Mistakes and Imperfections

Effective leaders are supposed to be continual learners. Mistakes in goals and tactics furnish good opportunities for learning. My seminar students have often chastised me, and properly so, for employing only leadership illustrations with a happy ending. "Tell us about mistakes and miscalculations," they urge. My assessment of effectiveness must include some notable disappointments. Any record of colleague encouragement and development must be placed alongside those personnel decisions where I mismatched talent to task. As previously mentioned, we did not raise as much private money as we could have because I failed to make an earlier, more intense, and more personal investment in this goal. We failed to get private residence halls built on campus (the university was prohibited by statute from having publicly built residence halls) because I failed not in intent but in imagination. The new chancellor at LSU Shreveport achieved this goal in his first year by the simple expediency of putting out a call for proposals.

As noted earlier, I served as interim chancellor of LSU Baton Rouge for eight months. I navigated with reasonable success the waters of big-time budgets and athletics, only to run aground on the question of who would be admitted to kindergarten in the campus school. My support for what I took to be a reasonable change in admissions policy to the campus kindergarten turned out to be an action with thorny civic and political consequences. The concern of board members, political leaders, and business executives over who would gain access to the fifty-five seats in the kindergarten turned out to be more intense than interest in the purchase of football tickets! There were big alligators in the Louisiana waters of that decision bayou.

Toward the end of my service as chancellor at LSU Shreveport, some faculty and community leaders grew concerned about my long-term commitment to the campus, as I had been a candidate for two other presidencies (one in my eighth year of service and one in my ninth). I withdrew from the first search and failed to catch the ring on the other (leadership stories for another time and place). Some faculty members also felt that we needed to be more successful in private fund raising. Both of these concerns were legitimately linked to my leadership decisions.

The Friendship of Conscience

The evaluation of leadership balance sheets certainly belongs in the hands of those we serve, where time and other factors may swing the performance needle from its initial position. But that evaluation belongs in the hands of leaders as well, because our theory of effectiveness influences our approach to leadership and shapes the climate in which our colleagues will serve. Leaders will ultimately need the friendship of their own conscience.

None of these performance indicators is infallible. Popularity may be shallow and fleeting, less to be valued than a long-term expression of trust and begrudging respect from constituents. Involvement in the life of campus and community carries little meaning when done for show and symbolism rather than as a result of caring. Regional, national, and international visibility can be helpful—if we remember who pays our check each month. Longevity in office can be associated with definitive leadership achievement; it can also be found in mediocre records in which organizational waters flow smoothly but unproductively over time. The growth of an organization can be a legitimate testimony to leadership talent and energy but can also reflect environmental trends and conditions that have little to do with skill and talent.

In Emerson's essay "Self-Reliance," he writes, "Nothing is at last sacred but the integrity of your own mind. . . . Trust thyself, every heart vibrates to that iron string" (1929, pp. 138–139). The friendship of one's own conscience is not infallible, but it is essential in framing a philosophy of leadership effectiveness. In these chapters, my aspiration has been to accent those ideals that might guide the conscience of those holding learning organizations in trust.

Here is the conclusion. Leadership is a conceptual, moral, and performing art form. It is an integrating art form involving the orchestration of ideas, values, and skills. It is a venture in moral philosophy. Honor, dignity, curiosity, candor, compassion, courage, excellence, service—these are design ideals that have been established in research, examined in philosophy, and tested in practice. These are design ideals for collegiate leaders who aspire to create a reality of goodness and to construct a climate of effectiveness for the individuals and the organizations they hold in trust.

These ideals do not require collegiate leaders to forsake the beautiful edges of their personalities, the unique elements of style that make them memorable and credible. They do not require a foolish and Pollyanna belief that ignores the reality that both nobility and meanness are present even in collegiate climates. They do not require a slavish consistency that ignores the power of surprise and the salutary contribution of what I earlier described as "guerrilla goodness." They do not require a sterile and rigid spirit, a spirit never softened or strengthened by journeys of pain, failure, disappointment, and mistakes.

These design ideals will find their highest promise in the lives of those leadership artisans who have spiritual scars and calluses on their characters, the evidence of their having struggled with difficult moral issues, weighed contending moral calls that defy neat resolution, agonized over the conflict between their own conscience and the judgment of an opposing majority, and struggled to know what it means to answer the call of honor.

I have long admired the poetry of James Kavanaugh, an artist of thought and language, a wordsmith of great power and simplicity. The gift of his poetic talent furnishes an informing and appropriate ending for the theme of leadership effectiveness and for this volume.

Somewhere Along the Way

Somewhere along the way
    A persistent voice taught me I was in competition
      with every other man in the world.
I listened carefully
    and learned the lesson well.
It was not enough
    To find a loving wife and have average, happy kids,
    To see a sunrise and wonder at an eclipsing moon,
    To enjoy a meal and catch a trout in a silent,
      silver river,
    To picnic in a meadow at the top of a mountain

or ride horses along the rim of a hidden lake,
To laugh like a child at midnight
    and to still wonder about the falling stars.
It was only enough
    To be admired and powerful and to rush from
        one success to another,
    To barely see faces or hear voices, to ignore
        beauty and forget about music,
    To reduce everything and everybody to a
        stereo color pattern on the way to some new triumph,
    To rest in no victory, but to create new and
        more demanding goals even as I seem to succeed,
    Until finally I was estranged and exhausted,
        victorious and joyless, successful and ready
        to abandon life.
Then somewhere along the way
    I remembered the laugh of a child I once knew,
    I saw a familiar boy wandering joyously in the woods,
    I felt a heart pounding with excitement at the
        birth of a new day,
    Until I was in competition with no one and
        life was clear again.
Somewhere along the way [1982, pp. 64–65].

—Maybe If I Loved You More

References

"Administrator Stole $326,000 in Aid." *Chronicle of Higher Education,* Aug. 5, 1992, p. A4.

Alinsky, S. *Rules for Radicals.* New York: Random House, 1971.

Anderson, M. *Impostors in the Temple.* New York: Simon & Schuster, 1992.

Association of Governing Boards of Universities and Colleges. *Trustees and Troubled Times in Higher Education.* Washington, D.C.: Association of Governing Boards of Universities and Colleges, 1993.

Astin, A. *Achieving Educational Excellence: A Critical Assessment of Priorities and Practices in Higher Education.* San Francisco: Jossey-Bass, 1985.

Astin, H., and Leland, C. *Women of Influence, Women of Vision: A Cross-Generational Study of Leaders and Social Change.* San Francisco: Jossey-Bass, 1991.

Autry, J. *Love and Profit: The Art of Caring Leadership.* New York: Morrow, 1991.

Axelrod, R. *The Evolution of Cooperation.* New York: Basic Books, 1984.

Bacon, Sir F. "Essays, Civil and Moral." In C. W. Elliot (ed.), *The Harvard Classics.* New York: Collier, 1937.

Badaracco, J., Jr., and Ellsworth, R. *Leadership and the Quest for Integrity.* Boston: Harvard Business School Press, 1989.

Banta, T., and Associates. *Making a Difference: Outcomes of a Decade of Assessment in Higher Education.* San Francisco: Jossey-Bass, 1993.

Barnard, C. *The Functions of the Executive.* Cambridge, Mass.: Harvard University Press, 1938.

Becker, E. *The Denial of Death.* New York: Free Press, 1973.

Belenky, M. *Women's Ways of Knowing.* New York: Basic Books, 1986.

Bellah, R., and others. *Habits of the Heart.* Berkeley: University of California Press, 1985.

Bennis, W., and Nanus, B. *Leaders: The Strategies for Taking Charge.* New York: HarperCollins, 1985.

Birnbaum, R. *How Academic Leadership Works: Understanding Success and Failure in the College Presidency.* San Francisco: Jossey-Bass, 1992.

Blake, R., and Mouton, J. *The Managerial Grid.* Houston, Tex.: Gulf Publishing Company, 1964.

Block, P. *Stewardship.* San Francisco: Berrett-Koehler, 1993.

Bloom A. *The Closing of the American Mind.* New York: Simon & Schuster, 1987.

"Board Fires President Amid Campus Turmoil." *Chronicle of Higher Education,* Nov. 25, 1992, p. A4.

Bogue, E. "One Foot in the Stirrup." *Phi Delta Kappan,* Apr. 1972, *52*(8), 506–508.

Bogue, E. "The Flogging of Theagenes." *Vital Speeches,* July 15, 1984, *50*(19), 596–599.

Bogue, E. *The Enemies of Leadership.* Bloomington, Ind.: Phi Delta Kappa, 1985.

Bogue, E. *A Journey of the Heart.* Bloomington, Ind.: Phi Delta Kappa, 1991.

Bogue, E., Folger, J., and Creech, J. *Assessing Quality in Higher Education: Policy Actions in the SREB States.* Atlanta, Ga.: Southern Regional Education Board, 1993.

Bogue, E., and Saunders, R. *The Evidence for Quality: Strengthening the Tests of Academic and Administrative Effectiveness.* San Francisco: Jossey-Bass, 1992.

Bok, S. *Lying.* New York: Random House, 1978.

Bolman, L., and Deal, T. *Reframing Organizations: Artistry, Choice, and Leadership.* San Francisco: Jossey-Bass, 1991.

Boyer, E. *College: The Undergraduate Experience.* New York: HarperCollins, 1987.

Bracey, G., and others. *Managing from the Heart*. New York: Delacorte Press, 1990.

Brecht, B. *Galileo*. New York: Grove Weidenfeld, 1966.

Burns, J. *Leadership*. New York: HarperCollins, 1978.

Caen, H. "Gamut from Ho to Hum," *San Francisco Chronicle*, Aug. 25, 1993, p. 6.

Cahn, S. *Saints and Scamps: Ethics in Academia*. Totowa, N.J.: Rowman and Littlefield, 1986.

Carnegie Foundation for the Advancement of Teaching. *Campus Life: In Search of Community*. Princeton, N.J.: Carnegie Foundation for the Advancement of Teaching, 1990.

Charmley, J. *Churchill: The End of Glory*. London: Hodder & Stoughton, 1993.

Cleveland, H. *The Knowledge Executive*. New York: Dutton, 1985.

Cohen, M., and March, J. *Leadership and Ambiguity: The American College President*. New York: McGraw-Hill, 1974.

Colby, A., and Damon, W. *Some Do Care*. New York: Free Press, 1992.

Commission on Colleges, Annual Report 1991. Atlanta: Commission on Colleges, Southern Association of Colleges and Schools, 1991.

Cook, A. "Magna Cum Fraud." *GQ*, Aug. 1992, *8*, 185–202.

Cordes, C. "Angry Lawmakers Grill Stanford's Kennedy on Research Costs." *Chronicle of Higher Education*, 1991a, *37*(27), A27.

Cordes, C. "Stanford U. Embroiled in Angry Controversy on Overhead Charges." *Chronicle of Higher Education*, 1991b, *37*(21), A20.

Cousins, N. *Head First: The Biology of Hope*. New York: Dutton, 1989.

Covey, S. *Principle Centered Leadership*. New York: Summit Books, 1990.

Csikszentmihalyi, M. *Flow: The Psychology of Optimal Experience*. New York: HarperCollins, 1990.

D'Souza, D. *Illiberal Education*. New York: Free Press, 1991.

Davies, P. *God and the New Physics*. New York: Simon & Schuster, 1983.

Delderfield, R. *To Serve Them All My Days*. New York: Simon & Schuster, 1972.

Deming, W. *Out of the Crisis*. Cambridge: Massachusetts Institute of Technology, 1986.

Depree, M. *Leadership Is an Art*. New York: Doubleday, 1989.

Depree, M. *Leadership and Jazz*. New York: Doubleday, 1992.

Dewey, J. *Moral Principles in Education*. Carbondale: Southern Illinois University Press, 1975.

Dibiaggio, J. "The President's Role in the Quality of Campus Life." *Educational Record*, Summer–Fall 1989, pp. 8–12.

Drucker, P. *The Effective Executive*. New York: HarperCollins, 1966.

Dubos, R. *Celebrations of Life*. New York: McGraw-Hill, 1981.

Emerson, R. *The Complete Writings of Ralph Waldo Emerson*. Vol. 1. New York: Morrow, 1929.

Epstein, J. *Ambition: The Secret Passion*. New York: Penguin Books, 1980.

Etzioni, A. *The Spirit of Community*. New York: Crown, 1993.

"Ex-Administrator Indicted for Embezzlement." *Chronicle of Higher Education*, Dec. 2, 1992, p. A4.

Festinger, L. *A Theory of Cognitive Dissonance*. Evanston, Ill.: Row Peterson, 1957.

Fiedler, F. *A Theory of Leadership Effectiveness*. New York: McGraw-Hill, 1967.

Fisher, J., and Tack, M. (eds.). "Leaders on Leadership: The College Presidency." *New Directions for Higher Education*, no. 61. San Francisco: Jossey-Bass, 1988.

Fisher, R., and Ury, W. *Getting to Yes*. New York: Penguin Books, 1981.

Florida Board of Regents. *State University System of Florida Master Plan, 1988–89 and 1992–93*. Tallahassee: Florida Board of Regents, 1988.

Frankl, V. *Man's Search for Meaning*. Boston: Beacon Press, 1959.

Galbraith, J. *A Tenured Professor*. Boston: Houghton Mifflin, 1989.

Gardner, J. *No Easy Victories*. New York: HarperCollins, 1968.

Gardner, J. *Excellence*. New York: Norton, 1984.

Gardner, J. *On Leadership*. New York: Free Press, 1990.

Garvin, D. *Managing Quality*. New York: Free Press, 1988.

Gibran, K. *Sand and Foam*. New York: Knopf, 1973.

Gilbert, M. *Churchill: A New Life*. New York: Holt, 1991.

Gilley, J., Fulmer, K., and Reithlingshoefer, S. *Searching for Academic Excellence*. New York: Ace/Macmillan, 1986.

Gilligan, C. *In a Different Voice: Psychological Theory and Women's Development*. Boston: Harvard University Press, 1982.

Gordon, A. *A Touch of Wonder*. Old Tappan, N.J.: Revell, 1974.

Graff, G. *Beyond the Culture Wars*. Chicago: University of Chicago Press, 1993.

Green, M., and McDade, S. *Investing in Higher Education: A Handbook of Leadership Development*. Washington, D.C.: American Council on Education, 1991.

Greenleaf, R. *Servant Leadership*. New York: Paulist Press, 1977.

Guaspari, J. *I'll Know It When I See It: A Modern Fable About Quality*. New York: AMACOM, 1985.

Harari, O. "Internal Customer, R.I.P." *Management Review*, June 1993a, pp. 30–32.

Harari, O. "Ten Reasons Why TQM Doesn't Work." *Management Review*, Jan. 1993b, pp. 33–38.

Hawking, S. *A Brief History of Time*. New York: Bantam Books, 1988.

Heilbroner, R., and others. *In the Name of Profit*. New York: Doubleday, 1972.

Hersey, P. *The Situational Leader*. New York: Warner Books, 1984.

Herzberg, F. *Work and the Nature of Man*. New York: Crowell, 1966.

Hilton, J. *Good-Bye, Mr. Chips*. New York: Little, Brown, 1934.

Hitt, W. *The Leader Manager*. Columbus, Ohio: Battelle Press, 1988.

Hodgkinson, C. *Educational Leadership: The Moral Art*. Albany: State University of New York Press, 1991.

Hollander, E. *Leadership Dynamics: A Practical Guide to Effective Relationships*. New York: Free Press, 1978.

Huber, R. *How Professors Play the Cat Guarding the Cream*. Albany: State University of New York Press, 1992.

Hughes, R. "The Fraying of America." *Time*, Feb. 3, 1992, pp. 44–49.

Hutchins, R. "The Administrator." In R. B. Heywood (ed.), *The Works of the Mind*. Chicago: University of Chicago Press, 1947.

Ingram, R., and Associates. *Governing Public Colleges and Universities: A Handbook for Trustees, Chief Executives, and Other Campus Leaders*. San Francisco: Jossey-Bass, 1993.

Kanter, R. *When Giants Learn to Dance*. New York: Simon & Schuster, 1989.

Kavanaugh, J. *Maybe If I Loved You More*. New York: Dutton, 1982.

Kerr, C., and Gade, M. *The Many Lives of Academic Presidents*. Washington, D.C.: Association of Governing Boards of Universities and Colleges, 1986.

Kets de Vries, M. *Leaders, Fools, and Imposters: Essays on the Psychology of Leadership*. San Francisco: Jossey-Bass, 1993.

Koestenbaum, P. *Leadership: The Inner Side of Greatness*. San Francisco: Jossey-Bass, 1991.

Kohn, A. *Punished by Rewards*. Boston: Houghton Mifflin, 1993.

Kouzes, J., and Posner, B. *The Leadership Challenge: How to Get Extraordinary Things Done in Organizations*. San Francisco: Jossey-Bass, 1987.

Kouzes, J., and Posner, B. *Credibility: How Leaders Gain and Lose It, Why People Demand It*. San Francisco: Jossey-Bass, 1993.

Kuhn, T. *The Structure of Scientific Revolutions*. Chicago: University of Chicago Press, 1962.

Land, G., and Jarman, B. *Breakpoint and Beyond*. New York: Harper Business, 1992.

Leatherman, C. "Breach of Etiquette Costs President of Florida State U. His Job." *Chronicle of Higher Education*, Sept. 1, 1993, p. A21.

Lederer, R. *Anguished English*. New York: Laurel, 1987.

Lederman, D. "Ousted President Sues Trustees of Arkansas State University." *Chronicle of Higher Education*, May 11, 1994, p. A24.

Livingston, J. "Pygmalion in Management." *Harvard Business Review*, July–Aug. 1969, pp. 81–89.

Lombardo, M., and McCauley, C. *The Dynamics of Management Derailment*. Technical Report 34. Greensboro, N.C.: Center for Creative Leadership, 1988.

Lunsford, T. "Authority and Ideology in the Administered University." *American Behavioral Scientist,* May–June 1968, p. 6.

MacArthur, D. *Reminiscences.* New York: McGraw-Hill, 1964.

McClelland, D. *Power: The Inner Experience.* New York: Irvington, 1975.

Machiavelli, N. *The Prince.* Norwalk, Conn.: Heritage Press, 1955.

Magner, D. "Law Firm Goes to Bat for Campus Conservatives." *Chronicle of Higher Education,* Sept. 25, 1991, p. A5.

Magner, D. "A Charge of Anti-Semitism." *Chronicle of Higher Education,* Jan. 12, 1994, pp. A12, A17.

Martin, T. *The Jewish Onslaught: Dispatches from the Wellesley Battlefront.* Dover, Mass.: The Majority Press, 1993.

Maslow, A. "A Theory of Human Motivation," *Psychological Review,* 1943, *50,* 370–396.

Maslow, S. *Eupsychian Management.* Homewood, Ill.: Irwin, 1965.

Mayo, E. *The Social Problems of an Industrial Civilization.* Boston: Harvard Business School, 1945.

Mercer, J. "5 Community College Leaders Indicted in Ohio Contributions Scandal." *Chronicle of Higher Education,* June 24, 1992, p. A25.

Milgram, S. "The Dilemma of Obedience." *Phi Delta Kappan,* May 1965, p. 605.

Mill, J. *On Liberty.* New York: Liberal Arts Press, 1956.

Mitchell, S. (trans.). *Tao Te Ching: A New English Version.* New York: HarperCollins, 1988.

Morris, R. *The Edges of Science: Crossing the Boundary from Physics to Metaphysics.* Englewood Cliffs, N.J.: Prentice-Hall, 1991.

Morse, S. "Leadership for an Uncertain Century." *National Forum,* Winter 1991, pp. 2–4.

Mullen, J., and Roth, B. *Decision Making.* New York: Rowman and Littlefield, 1991.

Myers, I. *Gifts Differing.* Palo Alto, Calif.: Consulting Psychologists Press, 1980.

Naisbitt, J. *Megatrends.* New York: Warner Books, 1982.

Neumann, A. "Making Mistakes: Error and Learning in the College Presidency." *Journal of Higher Education,* July–Aug. 1990, *61*(4), 386–405.

"Official Is Reprimanded for Role in Sex Video." *Chronicle of Higher Education*, Nov. 11, 1992, p. A4.

Pascarella, E., and Terenzini, P. *How College Affects Students: Findings and Insights from Twenty Years of Research.* San Francisco: Jossey-Bass, 1990.

Pascarella, E., and Terenzini, P. "Designing Colleges for Greater Learning." *Planning for Higher Education*, Spring 1992, *20*, 1–5.

Paton, Alan, "The Challenge of Fear." In *What I Have Learned.* New York: Simon and Schuster, 1968.

Paul, J. *"You Dropped It, You Pick It Up."* Baton Rouge, La.: Ed's Publishing, 1983.

Peck, S. *The Road Less Traveled.* New York: Touchstone, 1978.

Peters, T., and Waterman, R., Jr. *In Search of Excellence.* New York: HarperCollins, 1982.

Polster, M. *Eve's Daughters: The Forbidden Heroism of Women.* San Francisco: Jossey-Bass, 1992.

Prather, H. *Notes on Love and Courage.* New York: Doubleday, 1977.

"President Resigns Amid Lawsuit Over Aid." *Chronicle of Higher Education*, Sept. 2, 1992, p. A4.

Reddin, W. *Managerial Effectiveness.* New York: McGraw-Hill, 1970.

"Richard L. Van Horn Will Get a $100,000 Bonus When He Retires from the Presidency at the University of Oklahoma Next Year, But He Calls It a 'Burden' He Wouldn't Wish on Anybody." *Chronicle of Higher Education*, Oct. 27, 1993, p. A17.

Roche, G. *The Fall of the Ivory Tower.* New York: Regnery, 1993.

Rosenthal, R. "The Pygmalion Effect Lives." *Psychology Today*, Sept. 1973, pp. 56–63.

Sagan, C. *The Dragons of Eden.* New York: Random House, 1977.

Schein, L. E. *Organizational Culture and Leadership.* (2nd ed.) San Francisco: Jossey-Bass, 1985.

Schlesinger, A. *The Disuniting of America.* New York: Norton, 1992.

Senge, P. *The Fifth Discipline.* New York: Doubleday, 1990.

Sergiovanni, T. *Moral Leadership: Getting to the Heart of School Improvement.* San Francisco: Jossey-Bass, 1992.

Seymour, D. *On Q: Causing Quality in Higher Education.* New York: ACE/Macmillan, 1992.

Shaw, G. *Pygmalion.* New York: Signet, 1972.

Shepard, H. "Responses to Situations of Competition and Conflict." In R. L. Kahn and E. Boulding (eds.), *Power and Conflict in an Organization.* New York: Basic Books, 1964.

Skinner, B. *Science and Human Behavior.* New York: MacMillan, 1953.

Smith, P. *Killing the Spirit.* New York: Viking, 1990.

Solomon, R., and Solomon, J. *Up the University: Re-creating Higher Education in America.* Reading, Mass.: Addison-Wesley, 1993.

"Stanford University Dean Resigns After Arrest." *Chronicles of Higher Education,* June 10, 1992, p. A5.

Stewart, J. *Den of Thieves.* New York: Simon & Schuster, 1991.

Sykes, C. *Profscam.* Washington, D.C.: Regnery Gateway, 1988.

Tack, M. "Future Leaders in Higher Education." *National Forum,* Winter 1991, p. 30.

Thomas, L. *The Medusa and the Snail.* New York: Viking, 1979.

Thompson, V. *Modern Organizations.* New York: Knopf, 1965.

Thompson, V. *Without Sympathy or Enthusiasm: The Problem of Administrative Compassion.* University: University of Alabama Press, 1975.

Tompkins, J. "The Way We Live Now." *Change,* Nov.–Dec. 1992, pp. 13–19.

Toole, J. *A Confederacy of Dunces.* Baton Rouge: Louisiana State University Press, 1982.

Townsend, R. *Up the Organization.* New York: Knopf, 1970.

Vaill, P. *Managing as a Performing Art: New Ideas for a World of Chaotic Change.* San Francisco: Jossey-Bass, 1991.

Walker, D. *The Effective Administrator: A Practical Approach to Problem Solving, Decision Making, and Campus Leadership.* San Francisco: Jossey-Bass, 1979.

Walton, M. *The Deming Management Method.* New York: Perigree Books, 1986.

Weiner, J. "Lavish Compensation Is Not Appropriate for Top Executives at Public Universities." *Chronicle of Higher Education,* Nov. 25, 1992, pp. B3–B4.

Wells, H. B. *Being Lucky: Reminiscences and Reflections.* Bloomington: Indiana University Press, 1980.

Wharton, J. "Does Anyone Know Reality?" In *What I Have Learned.* New York: Simon & Schuster, 1966.

Wheatley, M. *Leadership and the New Science.* San Francisco: Berrett-Koehler, 1992.

Winkler, K. "The Driving Force of Communitarianism Seeks the Middle Ground Between 'I' and 'We.' " *Chronicle of Higher Education,* Apr. 21, 1993, p. A12.

Zaleznik, A. *Human Dilemmas of Leadership.* New York: HarperCollins, 1966.

Zukav, G. *The Dancing Wu Li Masters.* New York: Morrow, 1979.

Index

NATIONAL UNIVERSITY
LIBRARY   SAN DIEGO

NATIONAL UNIVERSITY